Proposition 13 and Its Consequences for Public Management

CONTRIBUTING AUTHORS

Clark C. Abt, President, Abt Associates Inc.

Charles T. Araki, Rensis Likert Associates, Inc.

Philip Burgess, Executive Director, Western Governor's Policy Office, Denver, Colorado

Hale Champion, Under Secretary, Department of Health, Education, and Welfare

Marcia Claxton, Director of Information Research, Municipal Finance Officers' Association

Richard J. Davis, Mayor, Portsmouth, Virginia

Thomas Fletcher, Stanford Research Institute International

Elisha C. Freedman, City Manager, Rochester, New York

Edward Hamilton, Hamilton and Rabinovitz, Los Angeles, California

John J. Kirlin, School of Public Administration, University of Southern California

Mordecai Lee, Representative, State Legislature of Wisconsin

Rensis Likert, Rensis Likert Associates, Inc.

Keith F. Mulrooney, Executive Director, American Society for Public Administration

Selma J. Mushkin, Director, Public Services Laboratory, Georgetown University; Fellow, Woodrow Wilson Center for Scholars, Smithsonian Institution

John E. Petersen, Director, Government Finance Research Center, Municipal Finance Officers' Association

Paul L. Posner, Supervisory Program Analyst, Intergovernmental Relations Group, General Accounting Office

Robert D. Reischauer, Assistant Director for Human Resources and Community Development, Congressional Budget Office

Frank H. Sandifer, Public Services Laboratory, Georgetown University

James M. Savarese, Director of Public Policy Analysis, American Federation of State, County, and Municipal Employees

Charlie G. Turner, Public Services Laboratory, Georgetown University

Charles L. Vehorn, Public Services Laboratory, Georgetown University

Proposition 13 and Its Consequences for Public Management

Edited by Selma J. Mushkin

Published by
THE COUNCIL FOR APPLIED SOCIAL RESEARCH
with the assistance of

ABT BOOKS
CAMBRIDGE, MASSACHUSETTS

Library of Congress Catalog Card Number 79-65017

Printed in the United States of America

ISBN: 0-89011-536-2

Contents

Preface

Proposition 13 has become a slogan for public dissatisfaction with American social policy and government management. The California affair and its reflective actions in other states and on the federal level have been interpreted by the press as an expression of the average taxpayer's desire to cut back the size and scope of government social services, as well as their tax costs. This book tells a different story: taxpayers are indeed unhappy about taxes and the presumed inefficiencies of government, but most taxpayers do *not* want any major reductions in government services, nor do they believe that such reductions are necessary to reduce taxes. Most voters, including conservative voters, believe that the savings in government budgets and taxes can best be achieved by improving the efficiency of government, not by reducing its output of services.

The revision of the popular interpretation of Proposition 13 offered in this book is important reading for officials at all levels of government and for policy researchers planning and evaluating the government's responses to the taxpayers' revolt. Evidence is presented from survey research, policy analysis, and public administration projects concerning both the nature of the public's resistance to taxes and the sources of the problem of increased government costs. To reduce government services in the mistaken belief that this is what taxpayers want would be a serious error in policy because it would both further increase public dissatisfaction with government and divert attention from the major source of the problem in the public's view: waste and inefficiency in public services management.

This book is based on the proceedings of a conference on Proposition 13 held in Washington, D.C., in September 1978. It was sponsored by the Council on Applied Social Research (CASR), the American Society for Public Administration (ASPA), the Public Services Laboratory of Georgetown University, and partially funded by a grant to CASR from the Policy Development and Research Division at the Department of Health, Education, and Welfare. The conference organizers, Selma Mushkin and Clark C. Abt, were concerned about the apparently panicky response of many journalists to the California Proposition 13 vote and the danger of misinterpretation of its meaning for social policy planning. The conference was intended as a forum for exploring the actual sources, meaning, and consequences for public policy of this important event. We invited representatives from all levels of government and from the social policy research community to attend the conference. Participants included leading policy planners and analysts, ranging from city and state government officials to senior officials of the Department of Health, Education, and Welfare, the Department of Housing and Urban Development, and the Congressional Budget Office. Also in attendance were several experienced policy analysts and public opinion survey researchers who offered new data and insights into the meaning of Proposition 13 and its possible consequences for public management.

The book is organized into four sections. The first offers the federal perspective on the meaning of Proposition 13 and probable responses and nonresponses to it as reflected in the administration's social policy, its administering departments, and Congress. The second section describes Proposition 13 and its antecedents from the point of view of state and local government planners in California. In the third section the local government perspective is expressed by city officials and state administrators, as well as by researchers concerned with local response. The fourth section presents a discussion of several major public opinion surveys concerning Proposition 13. It is here that some of the most iconoclastic and revisionist interpretations of the real meaning of the event are presented.

Preparation of this book was made unusually difficult by the attempt (not always successful) to capture from transcribed tape recordings the substance and spirit of the informal panel critiques and audience debates following each presentation at the conference. The high standards of the authors also required an unusually extensive and protracted process of manuscript review and revision. For these reasons, publication has taken longer than originally intended. These publishing problems were resolved by the dedicated efforts of many members of the Council for Applied Social Research and the Abt Associates Inc. publications staff. Selma Mushkin and Violet Gunther organized the selections. Nancy Miner managed the editorial process. Mary Elizabeth McClure copyedited the final manuscript, Deborah Greene set the type, and Sura Steinberg managed production.

Finally I want to thank all those who participated in the conference whose contributions are not represented in this book. Special thanks go to Dwight Ink, President of ASPA, for the fine job he did as moderator of the first conference session.

Clark C. Abt
President
Council for Applied Social Research

CAMBRIDGE, MASSACHUSETTS

Part One
The Federal Role

Husbanding the Public Dollar

Hale Champion

I won't go into the history of California finances, although I can remember having visited Brookings some years back to talk about the urgent need for revenue sharing because the property tax was poisoning the well of public taxation in California. I was a prophet considerably before my time.

Let me state my assumptions about what happened, so that my reasons for some of my remarks will be clear.

First, the property tax has long needed drastic reform, especially in California, and the state never met the challenge, even when it had the opportunity, in the form of a major flow of surplus revenues, to do so. I share some responsibility for creating this opportunity. I helped narrow the income tax brackets. We did not anticipate that these narrowed brackets would produce as much revenue as they did. We knew that narrower brackets would increase the revenue and that the increase ought to be used to reform property taxes. We never dreamed what a bonanza narrower tax brackets would be in a time of inflation.

Second, property owners are in many ways doubly pressured and scared by inflation. Under these circumstances people are less disposed to altruism and more disposed to look after themselves, even when they are already better off than others. They want desperately to cope with what is happening to them; they want to cut their costs. And they don't get to vote on the prices for anything except government.

Third, and perhaps most important, people are not satisfied with what they are now getting from government, for a lot of reasons — some good, some bad. They are not getting much help from government officials in sorting the good from the bad. The result is that those who are arguing for or seeking governmental reforms often end up contributing to what is already a massive tide of anti-government opinion.

These three assumptions help explain some of the things I want to say. There are obviously many other factors at work and many other ways to look at the reasons for Proposition 13. What I am saying about Proposition 13 is true, I think, of its offshoots around

3

the country. The question is what Proposition 13 means to public management.

Proposition 13 has not changed my view of what the agenda for public management should be. We all see in Proposition 13 the justification for what we have always believed — that if people would only do things our way, then Proposition 13 would not have happened or it will go away. Thus like most others who have the chance to comment on the impact of Proposition 13, I will say what I have always believed should happen and that Proposition 13 is another good reason to do it. Proposition 13 produces a greater sense of urgency; it gets people to pay attention. But fundamentally it describes what I would have said were the problems and agenda of public management before it passed.

It is important not to ignore the waves of feeling or even the slower kinds of political changes in our society. But it is even more important to have one's own sense of location and direction. I can best illustrate this point with a few examples. The former Governor Brown still supported fair housing after it lost two to one in California. My opinion of Proposition 13 has not changed because it passed. Proposition 13 has not assumed virtues that it did not have before it passed.

These remarks about Proposition 13 are intended as a backdrop for what I think public management ought to pay attention to. My suggestions are not necessarily in the order of their importance. They are influenced by my current experiences at HEW, and my examples are drawn from those experiences.

What most surprises me about HEW is that the single most important need in public management is for more management. HEW is dizzy with analysts and research. People become emotional, not about problems, but about which data to use. They argue about evaluations rather than problems. I exaggerate a bit, but my point is basically true.

About a year and a half ago at HEW there was not very much of what I would call management: the attempt to shape institutions to the needs for social protections and adjust the programs to the problems over time. Everybody was trying to design major policy, if possible, by the numbers. Enormous effort went into making decisions automatically by the data, verified before there had been any experience with these programs and evaluated afterward in terms of the numbers, without looking at the problem in a more common, direct, reportorial, experiential way — in a manager's way.

I think that HEW is still staggeringly far from paying much attention to management, to what people can do in shaping solutions to problems, apart from endless references to sets of data. I am frequently told that nothing can be done about a given problem because the right data sets are not available. I cannot remember a more emotional experience for an HEW staff than their discussion of how to aggregate hospital discharge data. Now, we all have beliefs that make us emotional. But people who are trying to bring about social improvement in this country have become preoccupied with data.

I understand the sensitivity to the charges that we did not pay enough attention to side effects. Side effects need to be anticipated, but side effects now seem to be the main concern at HEW, the possibility that something may go wrong. The concern with side effects is itself a kind of side effect among young people interested in public management. They want to talk about their careers. They are twenty or twenty-one, and they are going to be doing something for forty-five years; they want to know now what they are going to be doing each one of those forty-five years. They have a craving for security, for protection from some external set of promises and data, that takes the fun and the challenge from work on public policy. I would like to reintroduce the notion that management is a risk-taking, judgmental enterprise requiring many skills but fundamentally depending on the character and opinions and abilities of the people involved in it. I don't find much of that attitude in HEW, although I hope it will become more prevalent. I believe that the major item on the agenda of public management is to restore that attitude, to develop self-confidence about what people are doing and to stop being defensive and security-ridden.

My second set of comments concerns the shaping of an institution and getting away from the numbers. A good example is the Professional Standards Review Organization (PSRO), which is based on the assumption that qualified professional people are needed — doctors or other health professionals in this case — to determine the appropriate uses of federal health services programs. I don't know anybody else who can do it, so I think that this assumption is probably safe.

Before PSROs were one and a half years old, an enormous evaluation study was undertaken. I am already trying to deal with the fallout — in Congress, in the executive department, in the White House — from the study of an organization that is barely in place, that nobody has had a chance to shape in any real fashion. Already I am hearing talk about the waste of money and cries of doom for a program that has barely begun. Everyone has been so conscious of the data in this program that almost no one has tried to get it running right.

Another message of Proposition 13 is that those in government should pay less attention to themselves. Our careers, our status, our pay, our aspirations, what works for us, how we like what we do — all these concerns have become pervasive in public service — in local government, state government, and federal government.

The public has sensed the status concerns of the public employee. These concerns are not just the results of demands by public unions. Most industries have unions; the unions have a function, an important function, and they are bargained with. The public senses that too many of us in government are here for our careers and ourselves and our priorities and that not enough are here because we have a major interest, a consuming interest, in what happens to the people of this country.

Another item on the agenda of public management is the passion for equity that has gone amok. Equity, like other ideals, is something to strive for. But since bureaucracy is developed on a pretense that there can be a perfect equity, most people in a bureaucracy strive to achieve a kind of equity in everything, because that is what the bureaucracy is supposed to do. Equity becomes a consuming passion, unless one can stop and say, that's going too far. One must stop at a given point.

The Federal Register could be about half its present size if there hadn't been pressure each time something changed to have somebody else come out exactly even or be treated exactly the same way. We are a diverse people; there are many cultures and societies in our midst. The attempt to treat all exactly alike is respectable but unrealizable. We ought to acknowledge that there are going to be differences. To pursue equity to its limit is in effect to regulate everybody. The people have a perception that regulation has gone too far. They do not perceive regulation as a result of a passion for equity, they perceive it as an attempt to tell everybody exactly what they can and can't do. And the perception of what is fair obviously differs from one person to the next.

The unbridled pursuit of equity has gotten government into a lot of trouble. We ought to pull back and concede short-of-perfect equity. We should try to respond to the desire for equity without trying to control too deeply, in too much detail, either governmental or private behavior.

I think we need to solve the problem of regulation, whether the problem comes in the form of a regulations crisis or in the form of enforcement problems. For example, it is desirable that people not be pushed out of the work force and that the federal government not take steps that produce that result. But whether the federal government should ultimately resolve the issue of retirement is a real question. How well can the federal government decide whether somebody who has just reached the age of sixty-five is able to work as well after sixty-five as he did before? We have constantly gone into areas where we cannot make decisions that will apply to enough people to justify the intrusion of the federal or even local government.

Government is asked to defend people's rights in a number of areas, some very important rights, to end some important discriminations. But we end up trivializing our effort. We try to assure women an equal place in society, and we end up processing complaints because a group of cheerleaders cheered more loudly for the boys than they did for the girls. We try to assure the handicapped access to public buildings, and we almost end up making a small library in Iowa provide access for handicapped people when there are none in the town.

The trivializing demeans the major objectives, the attempts to eliminate great inequities. We ought to try to focus on the major inequities and avoid being sidetracked by this trivialization. Until we manage that, we are going to have many problems in public management.

I think we are going to have to organize — not in any highly structured way, but in an open way — the relationships among various levels of government jurisdictions.

We have talked about different ways of doing this, but we haven't reached any consensus. We have found some interim solutions; some have been good, some have not worked at all.

I think this administration and this president have probably done more to encourage that organization than anybody yet realizes. One of the real potential successes of the Carter administration is improved intergovernmental relationships and coordinated activity.

Proposition 13 is going to put some pressure on intergovernmental activities, but I don't think it is an unhealthy pressure. The pressure was there before, and Proposition 13 is going to call greater attention to it.

I can describe several things that we have done at HEW which indicate that there are ways to improve relationships and operational conditions at all levels. We have to stop looking simply at the levels of government; we have to look instead at programs and functions and let them adjust, not to political levels, but to the most natural or best way of carrying out a given function. This prescription is easy, broad, general. But we are beginning to find ways to fill it. I am not yet sure that we can persuade Congress that we ought to be allowed to, but we are making progress.

HEW sometimes reminds me of the seven buried cities of Troy. I don't think that any secretary has lasted longer than three years, three months. Each secretary had some notion of how to deal with the complexities of HEW, so artifacts of old administrations and ways of doing things are found at each level.

Richardson had the old massive monolith, a huge planned program, splendid, elegant, intelligent even. Yet it required so much manpower and so many resources to keep it going that it couldn't do anything. The minute conflict entered the picture, all progress ceased.

What we have tried to do this time is recognize that programs do all sorts of things, in different ways. We have three or four hundred different programs, ranging in size from Social Security, which has ninety thousand employees and spends over $100 billion, to some relatively small programs. Each one ought to be run as a separate program with its own integrity and its own method of operation. Instead of giving regional personnel the status of minisecretaries to run everything in their domain, we have made the program people responsible for program, wherever it is carried out.

Personnel in the regional offices still have important responsibilities. One is that they do service delivery assessments in the interests of the clients. These assessments are not careful, measured evaluations; they are attempts to go into the field and find out how people visualize the program. Their purpose is not to determine the real outcomes, measured scientifically, but to find out how people think and feel about the program, the people they are dealing with, and the way they are being dealt with. This type of assessment is working very well. The people are asked for their views and are pleased to be asked. They don't have to fill out questionnaires, they don't have to prove what they are saying; they simply give their anecdotal view.

A lot of other things have to be brought into the ultimate assessment. But the very fact that we have asked those people — not just the direct clients but also state and local governments and others involved in the process — and that we are looking at the program in their terms has made an enormous difference in our relationships and in the effectiveness of the service delivery. The people in the field, I think, now feel that we have given them something in addition to measurement techniques to ascertain when their own programs have accomplished something. Again, each program has its own set of aspirations and outcome measurements.

These changes are beginning to make field operations and their relationship with state and local government — to the extent that we have had a chance to test and observe the relationship — much more successful, much better than they were before. At least that is what I am told. I will know better when I get some additional assessments whether the relationship is better.

But the point I want to come back to is that people don't understand the governmental system; they don't understand the jurisdictional problems; they look at public management in functional terms. We need to talk to them in functional terms and we need to perform in these ways, so that they can see a program as a program. They don't care whether it is a local, state, or federal responsibility or how it is divided, as long as it works fairly well and in some integrated fashion.

The final thing that needs to be on our agenda is a sense that we are as concerned about the details of carrying out programs, the husbanding of the public dollar, as we are about their success. I am willing to say that Proposition 13 emphasizes this.

Public managers have two public responsibilities. They have a responsibility to the people who pay for programs and responsibility to the people served by programs. Those two interests will always conflict somewhat. In the Social Security Administration these two responsibilities have not been in the appropriate tension. The Social Security Administration has a great tradition of public service, but it has not been as concerned with the taxpayer as it should be. I don't want to suggest that the administration should pay less attention to the program's beneficiaries, but the managers need to pay more attention to the tax side.

A classic illustration of the need to keep these responsibilities in tension is the student aid program. Until last year the federal government made no effort to collect on defaults. Many students never received letters, never received any indication that the federal government cared about having those loans repaid. This neglect reveals a major failure of responsibility by people in government. The law made this aid a loan, not a grant. The program was good, but it was abysmally administered.

We need to pay attention to productivity, to outcomes, to measuring outcomes, to understanding what we are trying to do, and to find some way to ascertain whether we are doing it. In some programs measuring productivity is taken for granted. In others it has never occurred to the administrators. The Office of Civil Rights is an example. They had a huge backlog and requested more staff. But they had no idea how many cases each staff member closed per year. When we analyzed case handling over the previous year, we found out that each investigator was handling three cases a year.

The number is now twelve. Our projections indicate that it will soon be eighteen. The staff are pleased that they have been given some way of measuring their work. Obviously the number of cases handled says nothing about the quality of the handling. Quality has to be watched and monitored. But the staff needed some sense of whether they were making progress.

Each program has a different course to follow. In a health program mortality and morbidity can be measured only over a long period. But some interim measures can reveal a good deal and can ultimately have some effect on mortality and morbidity.

We put together a program on immunization last year, and within the first twelve months immunizations had greatly increased. We had the lowest measles year on record, right after one of the worst measles years in recent periods. This record was the result of setting targets, setting productivity goals for people involved in these efforts. The first thing we heard when we started was that people cannot be told what to do, that there are other ways to motivate people. But it is possible to set goals for others. Some goals they cannot set themselves, and some require marketing to persuade people to adopt these goals. And you can measure results, even of what other people do as a result of your efforts to persuade them to do it.

What I say today is probably what I would have said a year ago, before Proposition 13. Anything that makes us assemble, get together, and talk about public management and what is wrong with it and what ought to be done about it, with some sense of urgency, isn't all bad. And that is about the only good thing I have to say about Proposition 13.

Intergovernmental Responsibility for Meeting the Equity Considerations of Proposition 13: The Federal Role

Robert D. Reischauer

Those concerned with strengthening the horizontal and vertical equity of the public sector cannot be sure whether Proposition 13 and its relatives will be a boon or a bane. The feasibility or desirability of federal intervention to ameliorate instances in which the repercussions of Proposition 13 undermine equity are even less clear. Nevertheless Proposition 13, its progeny, and the actions that legislatures and governors are taking to ward off strong limits on government spending and taxing could raise important considerations of equity. This paper describes several possible equity-related effects of Proposition 13-type movements and then discusses the appropriateness of federal actions in these areas.

Taxation

The most obvious area in which to begin a discussion of the implications of Proposition 13-type actions for equity is taxation. If Proposition 13 is taken to mean limitations on local property taxes and an increased reliance on state-level taxes, such as sales and income taxes, then Proposition 13 could have a negative impact on vertical equity but a positive impact on horizontal equity. This latter possibility arises because, for families with a similar ability to pay (those with similar incomes), property tax burdens vary far more across the jurisdictions of a state than do sales or income tax burdens. A reduction in property taxes and increased dependence on sales, income, and other state-level taxes will therefore lead to a more uniform sharing of the costs of providing public services. But if arbitrary limitations are placed on the rate at which property assessments can rise, as they were .in the California initiative, new and even greater horizontal inequities might soon characterize the property tax. In post-Proposition 13 California property assessments will be allowed to increase by no more than 2 percent per year until a property is sold. At that time the assessment will be adjusted to reflect the market value of the property. Thus if real estate prices rise by 10 percent per year, a house sold in 1984 will pay twice as much in property taxes as a neighboring house of identical value that has not changed hands since 1975.

The federal government can do little about inequities of this sort. They have existed for years in many states. The U.S. Supreme Court might find the assessment rules under Proposition 13 unconstitutional, but the California Supreme Court decision does not offer much hope.

Massive property tax cuts, such as those in California, might provide the greatest benefit to the wealthiest and highest-income segments of society. I do not wish to debate conflicting views concerning the incidence of the property tax, but let me induce some skepticism about the much-heralded regressivity theory by citing some statistics on the California situation.

First, 14.7 percent of its $6.4 billion reduction in property taxes will accrue to the owner of agricultural land — and in California that owner is not the struggling small farmer. Another 29.9 percent will accrue to owners of commercial and industrial property. Some of the tax savings accumulated by the owners of such property might be passed on in the form of lower prices to consumers, but such a reduction is unlikely in the short run, given the uncertainty surrounding the future tax situation in California. Just over a third (36.5 percent) of the California tax cut will go to home owners. However, more than half that amount (54.1 percent) will accrue to families with incomes over $20,000, and only 26.2 percent will go to home owners with incomes under $15,000. Rental property will receive 18.7 percent of the total tax relief. Although over 70 percent (72.9 percent) of the relief for rental properties will go to units housing families with incomes under $15,000, there is no assured mechanism by which the savings to the landlord will be passed on to the tenants. This is especially true in tight housing markets, which seem to characterize California.

The federal government could try to ward off Proposition 13-type property tax cuts by instituting tax reforms that channel relief in a more progressive way. Some have long urged that the federal government institute a federal circuit breaker program or at least initiate a program to share the costs of state property tax relief efforts. I believe that these proposals are doomed to failure because it is impossible to design an equitable program of federal property tax relief in a nation having so much interstate variation in property tax burdens. For example, per capita property taxes in Alabama are roughly $60; in Massachusetts they exceed $500. Shortly after the original Serrano decision, the Nixon administration made a valiant effort to develop a way in which the federal government could reduce reliance on property taxes to finance elementary and secondary education. After many months of hard work, this effort failed to produce even a well-defined proposal.

Some Californians have made an audacious suggestion for federal action, which they think would enhance post-Proposition 13 tax equity. As a result of the cut in property taxes, California's property owners will have smaller itemized deductions and its businesses will have lower expenses to list on their federal tax returns. Proposition 13 will therefore increase their federal tax liabilities. Federal revenues from California's individual and corporate taxpayers will rise by an estimated $1 billion to $1.5 billion per year. Some have suggested that this windfall be returned to California. Although this proposal might seem reasonable if one lives in California, its rationality wears thin by the time the Nevada border is reached. By the same logic, Alabama should ask for tens of billions of dollars in "reparations" to compensate for the added federal taxes its residents have paid over the last fifty years because of low tax rates in that state.

Proposition 13 generates another tax-related federal policy issue. Some federal grant programs include tax effort in their distribution formulas. California and other states that are reducing their tax efforts may try to remove or weaken their importance in grant formulas. If one thinks that tax effort factors have improved the distributional equity of federal aid, steps should be taken to prepare a counterattack.

Spending

Proposition 13-type tax cuts are clearly going to have significant effects on spending. Services will have to be cut. Supporters of Proposition 13 appear to understand this fact and are willing to back a move toward a smaller government sector. From the standpoint of equity the salient questions are, What services will suffer the greatest cutbacks? and, Will services for the poor, the handicapped, minorities, and others who lack political clout be disproportionately slashed?

Only time can answer these questions. In California the day of reckoning has been postponed by the state's massive surplus. However, even in California, the evidence is not auspicious. California has tended to hold harmless basic services directed at the middle class or the majority of the population. For example, elementary and secondary education will be largely unscathed, because the state is distributing a large amount of new aid next year, which will provide school districts with about 90 percent of their expected fiscal 1978-1979 budgets. Although summer schools and some special programs will have to be trimmed, basic education will continue much as planned before the passage of Proposition 13. However, state categorical aids were cut back by 10 percent when the state instituted its economy moves. That cut will affect a number of state-financed redistributive programs such as the program for disadvantaged youth education, compensatory education, special reading programs, bilingual education programs, child nutrition programs, and urban impact aid.

Provisions in the state bail-out laws also ensure that basic police and fire services will not be reduced. The mandate that jurisdictions receiving state aid maintain their existing levels of protective services implies budget cuts in other services. Fire districts have already received almost all the money set aside to compensate special districts for their lost property tax receipts. Library, water, waste disposal, and recreational districts, among others, will therefore have to institute severe service cutbacks. Whether this pattern of cutbacks disproportionately affects the poor and underprotected is not clear. However, the action that California recently took in the area of welfare is clearly unequitable. To save state monies, California cancelled the 7.55 percent cost-of-living increase in welfare benefits that was scheduled to occur this past July.

In California and in other states that pass spending and taxing limitations, public employees are likely to be a target of budget cutters. Wage and hiring freezes are easy ways to reduce spending while maintaining service levels, at least in the short run. At one time freezing state and local employee wages would have hurt one of the lowest-paid segments of the American labor force. Many state and local workers, such as sanitation workers in the South and hospital workers, are still woefully underpaid. On the whole, however, this is no longer the case; public employees are now earning wages that are equal to, if not a bit higher than, those of all workers (see columns 1 and 2 of table 1). Moreover a very high proportion of state and local workers belong to multiple-earner families. State and local employees are far better off in terms of family income than are workers in general (see columns 3 and 4 of table 1). A one- or two-year wage freeze in the state and local sector might therefore cause less hardship than a similar freeze in some other sectors of the economy. Nevertheless wage increases in the state and local sector over the past few years have not kept pace with those in private industry.

Hiring freezes and layoffs, which are likely to result from Proposition 13-type actions, could signal a marked decline in job opportunities for the low-income and disadvantaged segments of the

Table 1. Distribution of All Workers and of State and Local Government Workers by Earnings and by Total Family Income

| | By Earnings | | By Total Family Income | |
| | | | | |
Income and Earning Range	All Workers	State and Local Workers	All Workers	State and Local Workers
$ 1-$ 4,999	40.4%	35.0%	20.9%	7.1%
$ 5,000-$7,499	14.4	13.7	12.1	7.6
$ 7,500-$9,999	12.1	14.7	11.1	9.9
$ 10,000-$ 12,499	11.3	14.0	10.9	11.0
$ 12,500-$ 14,999	6.5	8.1	9.1	10.6
$ 15,000 +	15.3	14.6	36.0	53.9
Total	100.0%	100.0%	100.0%	100.0%

Source: Estimates from the Survey of Income and Education, U.S. Bureau of the Census, 1976.

population. The state and local sector has been one of the most
dynamic job markets in an otherwise sluggish economy. During this
decade employment in the state and local sector has grown 50 percent faster than that in the economy as a whole; one of every five
jobs created since 1970 has been in state and local government. A
slowdown in hiring by state and local governments is likely to have
the greatest effect on women, minorities, and low-income, low-
skilled persons, because this sector has tended to hire dispropor-
tionate numbers of such persons. In addition, any layoffs caused by
tax and spending limitations are also likely to disproportionately
affect such persons, if workers with the least seniority are the first
to be let go (see table 2).

Increases in user fees and charges are a likely alternative to
service cutbacks. Although the state and local sector has been defi-

Table 2. Distribution of Selected Characteristics of Newly Hired and Long-
Term State and Local Noneducational Workers, 1976

	All Workers	Worker Hired	
		Over a Year Ago	Within the Last Year
Sex			
Male	58.1%	63.1%	48.7%
Female	41.9	36.9	51.3
Race			
White	82.1	83.3	79.3
Black	16.3	15.3	18.7
Other	1.6	1.3	2.1
Total Family Income			
$ 1-$ 4,999	6.6	1.7	14.8
$ 5,000-$7,499	7.9	5.5	12.0
$ 7,500-$9,999	10.6	9.8	12.1
$ 10,000-$ 12,499	11.6	12.4	10.4
$ 12,500-$ 14,999	10.4	11.6	8.4
$ 15,000 +	52.9	58.9	42.4

Source: Estimates from the Survey of Income and Education, U.S. Bureau
of the Census, 1976.

cient in its use of such devices, the introduction of user charges in some areas can raise equity problems. For example, the California trend toward imposing charges for swimming pools, school transportation, recreational facilities, and libraries might deny access to the very segments of society that have no private sector alternatives.

The ability of the federal government to influence the distribution of state and local government spending cutbacks is severely limited. The matching, maintenance-of-effort, and nonsupplementation regulations embodied in many federal grant programs are one area in which federal action seems desirable. There has been some fear that these provisions, which were not designed to cover situations in which a jurisdiction decided to drastically reduce public services, could result in cutbacks in federal aid that would compound California's difficulties. CBO and GAO studies suggest that in the short run California should not have its federal aid reduced significantly because of Proposition 13-related budget cutbacks.[1] Nevertheless federal officials should exercise as much leniency as the laws permit. CETA, Supplementary Security Income (SSI), urban mass transit, and some educational programs seem to be the programs in which leniency and a creative bending of federal regulations are most important if small local cutbacks are not to explode into larger reductions in federal aid.

Not all the effects of Proposition 13 on spending are likely to raise negative equity issues. A substantial reduction in local property taxes will lead to a larger state role in financing services now provided by local governments. Either services provided at the local level will be assumed by the state, or state aid to local governments will be increased. In all likelihood both will occur. An increase in the direct role of the state will reduce variation in the availability and quality of services across its jurisdictions. Similarly local tax differences are likely to be diminished. Increased state aid to local governments is also likely to lead in the same direction, because the distribution of state aid will have to reflect relative differences in need and fiscal capacity. In short, what Californians are beginning to call the "Serranization" of education will occur in all local services.

The signs of Serranization are already apparent in California. The state has agreed to finance both the state and the local shares of welfare for the next year, relieving counties of over $1 billion in

expenditures. The counties with depressed inner cities and impover-
ished rural zones will benefit most from this change. Although this
assumption of welfare costs is part of a temporary bail-out, it is
difficult to see how the financial responsibility for welfare can
ever be shifted back to the counties in California. The state will
distribute $2 billion in added school aid to compensate for lost
property tax receipts. Its temporary distribution formula can hardly
be considered an equitable long-run solution, but it is equalizing;
it provides high-spending school districts with enough money to
meet 85 percent of their planned 1978-1979 budgets and gives
low-spending districts enough to cover 91 percent of their planned
outlays. Thus Proposition 13 will help equalize local spending as
well as local tax rates and will provide a more equitable distribution
of welfare and school services.

The Private Sector

Taxes and spending are certainly the major arenas in which issues of
equity arise, but Proposition 13-type efforts will also spill out into
the private sector. I will discuss just one of the areas that they will
affect — housing. Proposition 13 and similar movements will probably undermine the ability of low-income and disadvantaged persons
to become home owners and to choose where they will live. Significantly lower property taxes will probably be capitalized into
housing prices, thereby making owner-occupied housing even more
expensive than it is today and even less affordable for young and
low-income families.[2] In California the price of new houses has been
raised even further by the increases in building fees and licenses
that California localities have imposed in their desperate search for
new revenue sources. The effect is already beginning to be felt.
July 1978 housing starts in California declined by 9 percent from
their June 1978 level, and in July 1978 they were even below the
levels of the year before.

Proposition 13 will also heighten the advantages of exclusionary
zoning practices. With limited revenues, few communities will be
interested in providing new housing for families that impose significant burdens on local public services. Low-income housing or housing for large families will be avoided. Because of the high initial

costs of newly annexed areas, annexation efforts are also likely to abate. Predatory competition for shopping centers and other sources of easy revenue will multiply. In short, the concentration of disadvantaged persons in central cities and their exclusion from the benefits of home ownership will probably be exacerbated.

It is difficult to determine an appropriate federal strategy for combating such repercussions of Proposition 13. Existing programs should be made to work better. But the record of the past cannot generate much hope that current programs will substantially increase the residential opportunities of minorities and low-income families.

Conclusion

Proposition 13 raises many equity issues but answers few. To the extent that equity is undermined by spending and taxing limitations, it will probably fall to the states to take compensatory action.

Notes

1. See Congressional Budget Office, *Proposition 13: Its Impact on the Nation's Economy, Federal Revenues, and Federal Expenditures* (July 1978), and General Accounting Office, *Will Federal Assistance to California Be Affected by Proposition 13?* (August 10, 1978).

2. To some extent this higher capitalization should be offset by the negative capitalization of service cutbacks into housing prices.

Proposition 13 and the Federal Grant System
Paul L. Posner

Passage of Proposition 13 by California's voters aroused widespread concern regarding the impact of projected budget cuts on the flow of federal grant funds to the state and its localities. In response GAO named three features of the federal grant system that could reduce funds to grantees experiencing budget reductions:

> *Matching requirements.* Sixty percent of federal grant programs require state and local governments to provide a specified share of grant costs as a condition for receiving federal assistance.
>
> *Maintenance-of-effort requirements.* To prevent fiscal substitution, many federal grant programs require grantees to maintain a prior fixed level of effort. Other programs require federal funds to be used to supplement, not supplant, nonfederal funds that would otherwise be available for the program. Thirty-seven of the fifty-two programs with over $100 million in fiscal year 1978 funding have maintenance-of-effort requirements.
>
> *Formula allocations.* Of the ninety-three federal formula grant programs, thirty-two reward higher grantee expenditures or taxing effort in allocating federal funds.

Clearly these provisions could affect the distribution of federal grant funds in a way that many would describe as perverse. Budget and program reductions at the state and local levels would trigger further service reductions in the form of reduced or discontinued federal funding. As governments decline fiscally, they frequently resort to increased taxation and reduced expenditures, which retard the area's economic development and lead to more serious problems. Thus it may not be surprising that the use of federal grants by fiscally troubled localities may also be ruled by this domino principle. Whether this contraction is desirable from a public policy standpoint is a significant question.

GAO's initial report on Proposition 13 *(Will Federal Assistance to California Be Affected by Proposition 13?)* concluded that it was too early to forecast the impact of Proposition 13 because federal funding depends on the fiscal decisions of relatively independent actors. The allocation of the state surplus, the budgetary decisions of each local government, and federal policy in administering or waiving grant provisions could mitigate the loss of federal funds. To clarify the actual effect, GAO has just embarked on an in-depth field review of selected California local governments to identify the actual size and shape of budget cuts, if any, and their impact on federal grant funding.

The GAO report also concluded that even if large local cuts occur, the impact of matching and maintenance-of-effort requirements could be blunted by flexibility accorded to state, local, and federal officials in implementing these provisions. While no one federal policy or set of criteria guides federal agencies in applying requirements, federal programs are guided by the primary goal: to ensure the allocation and obligation of federal grant funds to meet nationwide needs. The heavy hand of federal regulation can be counteracted by the overriding need of federal officials to spend their grant funds in the appropriate places. Indeed weak administrative implementation of the congressional intent behind matching and maintenance-of-effort requirements may be a blessing for the intergovernmental system itself.

Thus, for example, maintenance-of-effort requirements were designed not to penalize bona fide grantee fiscal reductions but to prevent contrived reductions to take advantage of federal funds. Nonsupplanting provisions allow the federal agency to make this determination, thus permitting continued federal funding for grantees with bona fide expenditure reductions. Of the thirty-seven programs with maintenance-of-effort requirements having national funding levels in excess of $100 million, fifteen permit administrative waivers. Matching can be waived for only five of the thirty-two matching programs over $100 million. However, the impact of the matching requirement may be mitigated because most programs allow existing in-kind resources and Federal General Revenue Sharing and other block grant funds to be used as a source of local matching.

Nevertheless some maintenance-of-effort and matching requirements are sufficiently stringent to impose hardship on local governments with large budget reductions. In several major programs reduction of one dollar of grantee effort triggers total withdrawal

of the federal grant. Similarly most programs with matching requirements do not allow waivers, nor does the rate usually vary to account
for differing fiscal situations. In a review of matching and maintenance-of-effort requirements, GAO uncovered a number of cases
of smaller or fiscally troubled localities who were unable to participate in federal grant programs because of prohibitive matching
provisions. Although matching serves as a fiscal litmus test to screen
out jurisdictions uninterested in participating in the program, these
jurisdictions may include those with the most need for the program.

Fiscally troubled grantees may also be deterred from participating in federal seed money grant programs, in which the federal
government provides funds for a limited time with the hope that
states and localities will eventually assume full program costs. Because the grant activates dormant local constituencies and fosters
new service dependencies, state and local governments are often
compelled to continue the project once federal funds expire. Because of the aggregate fiscal burden created, some state and local
governments have recently begun to reject participation in these
programs. California localities can be expected to look at these
grants with a newly jaundiced eye. According to one account, seed
money grants accounted for about $2 billion in 1977 federal grant
outlays and included such programs as community mental health
centers, drug abuse, law enforcement (LEAA).

Perhaps a more intriguing question provoked by Proposition 13
is not the effect of state and local fiscal crises on the federal distribution of funds but the federal contribution to these crises.
Indeed, as state and local resources diminish, the distribution of
federal funds could remain substantially unchanged. The economic
logic of the grant system may entice state and local governments in
fiscal decline to retain their federal grants at the expense of basic
services funded entirely from local sources, as a way to maximize the
dollar savings from their own sources while minimizing reductions
in program size or external funding. During times of resource scarcity, distortion of state and local budgetary priorities will intensify
to accommodate federal grant-related costs with shrinking local
resources. The GAO review of the impact of matching and maintenance-of-effort requirements found that local governments in
fiscal crisis disproportionately cut basic services while retaining their

matching-funds programs to avoid losing federal grants of lesser local priority.

Fundamental features of the grant system reward and encourage increased state and local spending while they penalize grantees experiencing bona fide expenditure reductions. Matching and maintenance-of-effort requirements, federally mandated costs and regulations, and the proliferation of categorical grant programs emerged during a twenty-five-year period of explosive growth in the state and local sector. Indeed for some time the state and local sector was the nation's leading growth industry, in terms of both expenditures and employment. It was plausible to assume that state and local governments could absorb federally spawned programs and costs as well as maintain or increase levels of traditional services.

Proposition 13 and the secular decline of some of the larger central cities may presage a new politics of resource scarcity at the state and local level. The dividend of fiscal growth may no longer be available to cushion the impact of the federal grant system. As a result, it is important to reexamine the assumptions and rationale underlying certain features of the grant system as part of the development of a new federal posture regarding state and local fiscal stability in an era of resource scarcity.

The grant features with the greatest impact on state and local costs include the following.

1. *Categorical grant proliferation.* Categorical grants stimulate state and local spending whether or not there are matching requirements. As state and local governments are enticed into participating in federally funded programs, dormant local constituencies become aroused and strengthened. As a result, a new set of resource demands and service dependencies is fostered, leading to higher nonfederal spending. When federal funding ends, state and local governments are frequently forced to absorb the full costs of these programs. State and local governments also incur nonfunded costs that result from new grant programs. For example, both federal highway and sewage treatment construction grants give heavy federal funding for new capital facilities, but state and local governments bear the full costs of operation and maintenance.

2. *Matching and maintenance-of-effort requirements.* Non-federal fiscal effort is stimulated or maintained in an increasing number of narrow categorical programs. Consistent with the logic of economics, program advocates at the state and local level successfully use matching to lever local spending in new areas in order to draw all available federal funds. As a result, some local governments have reported that their own resource allocations increasingly resemble the federal grant system. Consider, for example, a large local government in fiscal distress that must maintain effort in the following program areas.

> Law enforcement for LEAA funds
> Mass transit spending for Urban Mass Transit Authority operating subsidies
> "Services to meet the needs of the poor" for Community Action funds
> General education spending for large federal education programs
> Local public services for community development block grants
> Child nutrition under several federal child nutrition programs

3. *Mandated costs.* The federal government through regulation mandates costs that are not fully or even partially reimbursed, for example, compliance with Section 504 of the 1973 Rehabilitation Act, Unemployment Compensation coverage for all public employees mandated in 1976.

4. *Formula allocations.* Programs that reward increased grantee expenditure discourage more efficient and productive grantee operation of grant programs. In fact, expenditures become a proxy for performance, where some reliable output measures could be used instead.

Policy Dilemmas

Passage of Proposition 13 and its spread to other states pose several policy dilemmas for the federal assistance system. If resource scarcity becomes a permanent feature of the public sector, the following intergovernmental fiscal problems are posed for the federal assistance system.

1. Should the federal government continue to reward increases in the size of the state and local sector? Alternatively, should it remain neutral or actually encourage decreases? If expenditure reductions are encouraged through the federal grant system, is there a risk that federal funding will merely displace state and local funding, thus encouraging greater dependence on federal funds and less local autonomy?

2. Can the federal government tolerate decreased participation in grant programs developed to meet nationwide needs by state and local government undergoing fiscal retrenchment? Is the resultant distribution of federal funds skewed from areas or groups especially in need of federally funded services?

3. If this skewed distribution is to be rectified, should the federal government adjust grant requirements through waivers and other variances for all governments in fiscal distress? Or should policy distinctions be made between fiscal distress caused by secular economic decline and fiscal crisis brought about by the voluntary actions of wealthier communities? How should these distinctions be operationally determined?

4. If participation in grant programs begins to decline, should the federal government directly provide services for needy areas that cannot or will not participate in federal programs? What impact might this policy have on a federal budget that may also feel the force of taxpayer revolt?

5. How can emerging federal policies to shore up the fiscal and economic vitality of state and local governments through such efforts as general revenue sharing, countercyclical assistance, and emergency public works assistance be reconciled with federal grant requirements, such as matching and mandated costs, that exacerbate state and local fiscal pressures?

The Early Referenda and Federal Response

Donna Shalala

California has had a history of initiatives and referenda on the property tax and on financial reform. Anyone in California, elected or appointed official, who thinks that the people hadn't been sending messages should recall that California voters came very close in the Reagan Amendment in 1975 to passing a much more stringent, more difficult referendum than Proposition 13.

A number of referenda were on the ballot in California in the 1970s. The first of these efforts was encouraged by the assessor of Los Angeles County and eventually by Governor Reagan. These referenda established a pattern of political shifting in which high-income voters were beginning to vote against redistributive proposals, proposals that wanted to substitute the wider tax base of the state for the property tax.

California relied more heavily than other states on the property tax for financing services. While this reliance was declining in California, the decrease was not as dramatic as it had been in other places, and the percentages were still higher than those in other places. For example, between 1942 and 1975 California decreased its dependence on the property tax from 40 percent of all state and local revenues to 28 percent. During this period California relied on federal aid to an increasing extent, 18.6 percent in 1975 compared with 8.2 percent in 1942. It began to raise a greater proportion of its revenue from income taxes as well, 3.5 percent in 1942 compared with almost 9 percent in 1975.

Numerous other states have followed this trend, moving away from dependence on the property tax to federal aid and state income taxes. But California has always generated a large proportion of its general revenue from the property tax. In 1975 only four states, Connecticut, Massachusetts, Nebraska, and New Jersey, relied on the property tax for a larger proportion of their total general revenue than California; with the exception of Massachusetts, these other states did not levy the income tax until the 1960s.

The national average percentage of state and local expenditures provided by local governments is about 35 percent, but California's percentage is about 44 percent—again, higher than other places in the

29

country. Proposition 13 brings California's percentage more in line with many of the other major urban states across the country.

There are thus two points to bear in mind. One is that there's a political history in California about Proposition 13. While Proposition 13 has national implications that we have to be sensitive to, it has to be put in a narrower California context on the political side. The second point is that California was out of line with what other places were doing in terms of lowering the percentage of state and local expenditures that were paid by property tax expenditures.

In Washington we're still struggling to figure out the message of Proposition 13 that we're supposed to be translating into operating programs. Is the message that people are unhappy with the size of government? Is the message that we need to restructure who pays for the system? Is the message that those of us in Washington ought to trade off general revenue sharing for the targeting approach that many of us would prefer?

The message to us is far from clear, and we still have not sorted out which aspects require a response. I think that the debate will be held as the big federal programs, particularly those related to cities, come up for vote in the next fiscal year. There will be a major debate over the revenue-sharing and community development block grant programs.

Proposition 13 on balance affects federal government funding very little. All sorts of cost studies are going on to determine how Proposition 13 impacts on federal programs. For programs that require maintenance of effort Proposition 13 will result in a loss to California. For a long time the federal government built in those requirements to encourage state and local governments to undertake activities that they would not have ordinarily supported. To the extent that maintenance-of-effort measures continue to be built into particular federal programs, California will lose some federal money.

Cutbacks could obviously jeopardize federal funds where matching is required. There have been some attempts to determine where these cutbacks are going to be a serious problem. Cutbacks that affect individuals, actual cuts in employment, which require unemployment compensation, food stamps, additional welfare payments, will obviously cost the federal government some money.

We have looked with some care at housing programs, for example, Section 8. A lower property tax should slow the rate of rent increases, which, in turn, would reduce federal outlays. However, if California denies a cost-of-living increase to AFDC recipients, tenant contributions toward rent may be lower. If tenant welfare benefits are frozen, which will mean a real reduction in tenants' incomes, then federal operating subsidy payments to public housing projects will have to be increased. We estimate that the increase could be as much as half a million dollars. But we do not have exact figures yet because the authorities in California are still giving us their numbers.

We have talked at length about what we ought to be doing about California, and in discretionary programs the president has ordered federal agencies to help California state and local governments get through the crisis. But because of the surplus in California, the pressure has not been on federal agencies. We have felt great pressure to readjust federal programs to respond to Proposition 13. Federal agencies are waiting and feeling some anxiousness about what Proposition 13 means in terms of our projections on subsidy payments in California.

I may be more relaxed than some other people because I've been through the New York experience. We had warned the world that the cuts were going to be shattering, and there is no question that they were difficult, but we survived with less pain than anyone had anticipated without the surplus that California had. In New York we created our own surpluses.

What are we going to do about California? My own Office of Policy Development and Research at HUD has begun a monitoring effort to measure the effects of Proposition 13 in California. We need to anticipate whether some of HUD's programs will need restructuring if there are rapid cuts in state and local spending around the country as a result of a taxpayers' revolt.

We are looking carefully at the need for additional targeting of funds. Our approach is to look for ways to target in terms of need. To the extent that the California experience will create some inequities, there will be further targeting.

More important is the more fundamental research that is being done. On the capital issue the Urban Institute is expected to give us a report sometime next year. It is the first major study of the infrastructure needs of U.S. cities, a series of case studies of the larger cities. We expect to have a recommendation early next year. This recommendation will attempt to get the government to take a more precise look at the capital issue.

In addition, we will review pensions, both in the context of the president's effort and as an independent effort to get the numbers needed for comparable analysis and for projecting future pension costs. That study is expected to be funded in the next month or so.

Still more important is our search for ways of using the cruder instruments of government, tax policy and economic policy, to relieve state and local governments.

Finally, the president's requirement for use of urban impact statements, which are analytical tools, may help somewhat. In all new initiatives we will have for the first time in this coming budget process an analysis of the special impacts and some of the equity considerations. After we have finished analyzing the new initiatives, we intend to analyze the major federal programs and see what those initiatives are.

No one is looking for fresh, new approaches to respond to the messages that were sent in the vote in California. Those messages require answers to issues that many people have been talking about for years — the restructuring of the tax system, particularly the state and local tax system, and a rethinking of the allocation of functional and fiscal responsibilities. I do not know whether the result will be a restructured tax system or a reallocation of responsibilities. But it seems to me that the older approaches that so many have worked on for so many years are still the responses to the vote in California.

Part Two
The California Affair

Tax and Expenditure Limits: Proposition 13 and Its Alternatives

John E. Petersen
Marcia Claxton

The passage of Proposition 13, also known as the Jarvis-Gann initiative, by the voters of California, brought national attention to what has been termed a taxpayer revolt. Although the revolt had surfaced many times before, calling for limits on spending or rollbacks of taxes, it seldom enjoyed much success. However, conditions in California seemed to augur a momentous happening as the referendum drew closer. Many areas of the state had experienced meteoric increases in property values and tax bills. The state found itself with a massive (and consistently underestimated) surplus, and voters were clearly upset about the overall size, number, and quality of the programs of local governments. Furthermore, the proposed rollback of the property tax and restrictions on other taxes were simply stated, dramatic, and supported publicly by both colorful and prestigious personalities.

The tax and expenditure limitations as a group have been labeled TELs. But they are diverse in their design and implications. Most of those currently on the ballot or under debate do not promise to radically change state and local finance, although several would cause immediate spending reductions and almost all would curb any further growth in the public sector relative to the private sector. Furthermore, they vary greatly in whether they treat both the state and local levels or simply one, in whether they are targeted at general expenditures or revenues or are essentially property tax limits, in how much flexibility they permit for future growth, in provisions for overrides, in whether special items (such as emergency needs, grant-supported expenditures and debt service) are included.

This report first discusses the nature of Proposition 13 and its consequences in California and then considers the attributes of TELs more generally.

Tax Reform: California Style

California, the most populous state in the union with 10 percent of the nation's population, by passage of Proposition 13 last June chose to become the test tube for examining the effects of strong state-wide tax limitation. Although many factors undoubtedly entered into the amendment's resounding victory, the primary motivation was taxpayer outrage over spiraling property tax bills. Already a relatively high tax-effort state by most measures, California was routinely translating recent rounds of inflation in its property values into increased assessments and tax levies. Part of the problem stemmed from the fact that many jurisdictions were on a three-year or longer reassessment cycle. Thus in the face of rapidly rising property values, increases in property tax bills came in big chunks, as lagging properties were suddenly jerked up to current market values.

Whatever the technical explanations for overworking the property tax, the newspapers were filled with accounts about how tax bills were doubling and tripling. Taxpayers understandably feared that next year it would be their turn and that they would be taxed out of their homes.

After years of unsuccessful efforts, the proponents of tax reform and abatement in California suddenly found their cause in the ascendancy. The popular frustration over rising property tax bills was undoubtedly increased by the state's large — and consistently underestimated — revenue surpluses. The surplus was used effectively and correctly (at least for the time being) as a rationale for cutting local taxes without necessarily cutting vital expenditures. The inability of California state government to use the surplus to ease local tax burdens further infuriated the constituency. No doubt, too, various local concerns reinforced the sour mood of the taxpayers who felt compelled to "send a message to Sacramento."

What could not be clear to anyone at the time of its passage were the full implications of Proposition 13 for California governmental finance. These results are now working themselves out as the various provisions of that measure are being implemented by state and local legislative bodies and government officials, under the watchful eye of the courts.

The major provisions of Jarvis-Gann — along with their implications — are as follows.

Maximum property tax shall not exceed 1 percent of market value at 1975 levels. This limit on property tax revenues does not apply to taxes collected for repaying bonded debt approved by the voters prior to July, 1978. In other words, property taxes collected to repay outstanding voter-approved general obligation bonds are not affected by the tax ceiling. However, future debt service on general obligations would be part of the overall ceiling on property taxes unless secured by a "special" tax voted and approved by two-thirds of the qualified electors at referendum. These provisions have important implications for both outstanding debt and future borrowing powers of California local government.

Revenues from property taxes shall be apportioned "according to law" among the districts and counties. In California there are numerous special districts in addition to the general units of government. Almost every district and unit of government has relied on the property tax base, a situation that created a lot of overlapping tax rates. This means that counties, cities, school districts, and certain other special districts all set rates and collect their share of taxes on individual pieces of property. At the time Proposition 13 was passed, no existing law specified how property tax revenues under the 1 percent cap would be apportioned among the governmental jurisdictions.

The California legislature, in its emergency distribution of over $4 billion in state surpluses, set forth in the statute a proration of property tax receipts on the basis of historical averages. However, the distribution is temporary and a matter of statute, hardly providing a rock of revenue dependability for bondholders, among others. Future apportionments among the approximately thirty-eight hundred local government units will need to be worked out through litigation or some permanent legislative solution.

Property values are based largely on the assessments of March 1, 1975. Thereafter the maximum increase in assessed value permitted is 2 percent per year, except for new construction or parcels in which there has been a change of ownership. Here again, the amendment is beset with numerous definitional problems. It remains to be seen how the courts or the legislature will interpret this requirement. Clearly, however, a 2 percent rate of growth in assessed value will be far below the historical growth experience in property values. As a practical matter this will lead to a decreasing real burden of the property tax through the years for those who stay put. Furthermore, defining what will constitute construction or a change in owner-

ship and then devising a way to circumvent tax increases will undoubtedly be troublesome.

*Any new state taxes voted by the state legislature must be
passed by a two-thirds vote. No new real estate taxes may be imposed at either the state or local level. Local government may impose
"special taxes" but only by a two-thirds vote of the "qualified"
electors.* The substance of these provisions is to make the creation
of new property taxes impossible and the creation of other sources
of local government revenue — at least those that will be defined as
taxes — virtually impossible. Besides the heavier reliance on user
charges and fees that has already started, local governments will be
under pressure to use existing non-property-taxing authority to its
maximum.

The entire measure took effect July 1, 1978. The amendment
has come under immediate legal challenges and is under review by
the California Supreme Court on several grounds. If any particular
section of the amendment is held unconstitutional, the others will
remain in effect. The severability clause probably guarantees that
the critical provisions of Proposition 13 will pass a court test. Definitive answers to the legal questions remain several months — perhaps
years — away.

Emergency Bail-Out

The California Legislature moved rapidly to take much of the immediate sting out of Proposition 13's passage. Property tax revenues
were reduced by $7 billion (of a $30 billion total for all local government budgets in fiscal year 1979) by Proposition 13, but a quickly
enacted state aid package covered $4 billion of the loss, meaning an
average 9 percent rather than 21 percent reduction in revenues.
The aid was also designed to compensate partially for the differential
importance of the property tax by type of local government.

The state assumed $1 billion in local welfare costs outright.
In addition, education has become essentially state financed and
directed with little discretion for expenditure levels left to the
local level.

The state has set certain conditions on local receipt of state
surplus assistance. Among the major areas of increased state involvement in local government decision making are financial manage-

ment, service delivery, and labor relations. A major stipulation tied to the state-aid package is that local governments that show a surplus or reserves of more than 5 percent of total revenues will have their aid reduced by one-third of the excess amount.

County governments are mandated to tax up to 1 percent of the true market rate and perform other adjustments to their taxing and assessment procedures.

With respect to provision of public services, the law requires that police and firefighting services must be maintained at existing levels. Public health can be reduced only proportionately, and budgets are to be examined by the state.

State assistance will not be given to localities that give cost-of-living increases to employees or welfare recipients exceeding those given to state employees. (This voids any local contracts to that effect.)

To enforce these stipulations, California will necessarily require much stricter surveillance and financial reporting procedures. Budget elements (fire and police, surplus limit, public services) are subject to line-item review, with loss of state assistance as penalty.

County governments have gained additional control over special districts by virtue of the fact that the county board of supervisors will have broad discretion in allocating aid to special districts within the guidelines.

Even the most ardent apostle of tax cuts will probably agree that without massive infusions of state aid, many local governments would have had to cut muscle and bone, not just fat, from their budgets. The distribution of the state's surplus funds is cushioning the blow of Proposition 13 only temporarily. The real test is how expenditure cuts will be made and alternative revenue sources found to compensate for sustained reduction in property tax revenues as the 2 percent growth limit restricts the growth in the tax base below that needed to keep abreast of even moderate increases in expenditures due to inflation.

Borrowing and Capital Financing Problems

One vital area that has been turned topsy-turvy by passage of Proposition 13 is local government capital facility financing. Passage of the amendment not only jeopardized certain types of outstanding debt but left in its wake numerous problems for the future financing of capital outlays through borrowing, grants, and current revenues.

Because California continues to grow rapidly and because many areas of that state are maturing, capital expenditures for both new and replacement facilities are vital. Yet because many projects are postponable and are vulnerable to changes in financing sources, capital outlays will surely be one of the big losers in the push to economize.

The nationwide trend toward tax and expenditure limitations and property tax rollbacks means that the California experience and its impact on capital financing have an importance that transcends that state's boundaries. Proposition 13 has resulted in both immediate and long-term considerations with respect to California capital spending and an urgent need for a new strategy for public investment in that state.

Impact on General Obligation Bond Financing

Proposition 13 carried a specific provision that voter-approved general obligation debt approved before July 1, 1978, was exempt from the 1 percent tax levy ceiling. In other words, voter-approved local debt authorized before that date can rely on the traditional security of an unlimited ad valorem tax. Because it is likely that only a small amount of debt was authorized by the voters but unissued before July 1, 1978, most new general obligation capital financing in California will have to be supported by the proceeds from the 1 percent tax or by non-property-tax revenues. (Traditional revenue bond financing will probably not be affected by Proposition 13.)

Issuing general obligation bonds payable from such limited taxes will present numerous problems. Traditionally, the ultimate security behind local government general obligation bonds has been the pledge of unlimited property taxes. To substitute a pledge of property taxes or of non-property-tax revenues, assuming the latter would be authorized by voters, will require a new outlook by investors and new legal and financing techniques.

Regardless of the form of new general obligation financing that is used, a key problem will be providing sufficient future revenues to assure repayment. If local revenues are so tight that outlays for vital services (such as police and fire) and outstanding obligations (debt and pensions) will be impaired, then budgeting for future principal and interest payments will be even more difficult. The problem therefore involves finding not only new debt instruments for California cities but also an assured revenue stream to pay future debt service.

In the absence of new tax-supported debt instruments and sufficient revenue streams, the following paths are likely to be followed in financing capital facilities.

Greater reliance on the private sector. Local governments in California have been leaders in the use of special exactions, fees and subdivision dedications being required of new neighborhood development. While these have been criticized on grounds of equity and their impact on housing costs, Proposition 13 restrictions would seem to reinforce the trend toward them. Furthermore, as local governments come under increased revenue pressure, a probable tendency would be to spin off services that are now provided by the public sector into the private sector, which could lessen the need for local public expenditures for capital.

Greater use of fees and charges. Now in only moderate use in California, user charges and fees will prove to be an alternative source of revenues that can be used for capital financing. However, there are many constraints on the use of this source that need to be considered. First, the conversion of financing activities that are now supported on a property tax basis to a user charge basis will undoubtedly raise legal challenges, as well as practical administrative problems. Second, user charges will represent a limited and hence less secure form of revenue to support future borrowing so that borrowing costs will be higher. Third, the use of charges could have undesirable consequences for poorer and lower-income residents as more of the burden for charge-supported services is shifted to them.

Greater reliance on the state. The state of California may assume more of the financing burden for local facilities. By and large, California localities have had to assume the major burdens of public capital programs, and state debt burden is modest by national standards (the state is rated Aaa). A constriction in local borrowing could be overcome by state credit assistance through various loan programs, guarantees, or debt-service subsidies to local units. While this appears possible because of the state's high credit rating, too much help to local governments would dilute the state's ability to bear debt. Also because of the limitations placed on new taxes by Proposition 13, raising taxes to provide for capital grants to local governments or to assume present local expenditure responsibilities might prove difficult.

Impact on Outstanding Debt

In California, as elsewhere in the country, much local debt that relies either directly or indirectly on the property tax is not, in fact, voter-approved general obligation debt. Proposition 13's provisions adversely affected three major types of local securities:

Tax allocation bonds. Used for commercial and residential area development, tax allocation bonds rely on increased property tax revenues caused by the debt-financed development for their repayment. The rollback of property values and the capping of growth in assessed value has seriously jeopardized projects in midstream that are relying on much faster growth — and higher levels — of tax than are now allowable. About $1.6 billion in tax allocation bonds (over 250 issues) is outstanding. Standard and Poor's and Moody's have thus far withdrawn ratings on over $600 million of these bonds because of doubtful repayment. As part of the emergency aid, the legislature has provided a one-year $30 million appropriation to help avoid defaults in these bonds but has not taken any permanent action to bolster their security.

Lease rental bonds. Many units in California lease facilities from special districts that have been created solely for purposes of financing construction of that facility. The major attraction is that the debt so created comes outside the unit's debt limit and need not be voter approved. Approximately $1 billion of lease rental bonds has been sold where the leases are secured on property taxes. The reduction of property taxes has curbed funds available to make the rental payments in many units, but it is too early to say how many are endangered.

Other securities. There are numerous special assessment districts in California with about $250 million in outstanding bonds that rely, in the first instance, on special assessment revenues (usually from property taxes) but that also have a general obligation backing. These bonds, and therefore their repayment if taxes are needed, have come under the 1 percent cap.

In summary, it appears that $2 billion to $3 billion in outstanding California local debt of these varieties has come under a cloud. Most of it undoubtedly will weather the storm. But more definitive statements are not possible until an orderly review of security provisions and future revenue losses is undertaken. Most important, the use of these security types to meet future needs is dubious at best.

Potential Reduction in Capital Spending

The reduction in California capital spending is difficult to estimate in view of the lack of data currently assembled about use of proceeds and annual sales volumes. A reasonable estimate, however, in view of the importance of tax-supported borrowing is that approximately $400 million in annual local government capital outlays would be affected because of borrowing difficulties. Moreover, an unknown amount of related private sector capital investment (in redevelopment projects) would no longer be feasible.

But there are other important impacts for capital spending that will result from the increased pressure on current revenues. Generally, most units of government are expecting to experience a 10 percent decline in revenues this year (1979) and most likely a similar round of reductions in fiscal year 1980. An important way to cut expenditures is to postpone capital improvements, replacements, and — especially — maintenance. No numbers now exist on what these financial items currently contribute to California budgets. However, if that state's expenditure by character is somewhat similar to that found nationwide, 15 percent of total capital outlays is for equipment, land, or existing facilities. Also approximately 5 percent of the operating budget represents expenditures for maintenance. For example, reductions by one-half of their current levels of these

outlays would mean a $200 million reduction in local capital spend-
ing and a $400 million reduction in maintenance and repairs by
general units of government.

Another blow to local capital spending comes from the potential loss by California communities of federal assistance. In this
complicated area it is much too early to project the sum involved,
but there appear to be several points of exposure. Most federal
grant programs involve matching and maintenance-of-effort requirements, and an inability of government to raise its share through
borrowing or current receipts could lead to a loss of federal grants.
Furthermore a reduction in local tax effort will ultimately reduce
the share of formula grants.

Considering the Trade-offs

In light of these real and potential losses many local governmental
units will move to defer maintenance, abandon capital outlays, and
reduce "frills." While essential services, such as police and fire,
will be maintained at adequate levels (because of a requirement in
the emergency aid bill), amenities such as recreational and cultural
programs are likely to be cut, as are social service programs. Choices
of local government officials between what they can and cannot do
with scarce revenues are made even more difficult by the many
fixed costs that are part of each year's budget. These fixed costs —
pension contributions, debt service obligations, fuel costs, leases, and
state and federally mandated service — have already reduced the
fiscal flexibility of local governments. Ultimately, sustained reductions will come from employment, since the wage bill typically
makes up 70 percent of local government outlays.

Unfortunately the Proposition 13 plebiscite was not designed to
associate the resulting revenue cuts with specific expenditure reductions. Individual voters have their own perceptions of how money
can be saved. However, these same voters are likely to react strongly
if their bus route is cut, their park is closed down, or their youth
center is eliminated. It remains to be seen what course public sentiment will take. Disgusted with big government, the voter may con-
tentedly adjust to fewer, less comprehensive public services. On
the other hand, as the public pie grows smaller, the claimants are
likely to become combative.

To aid in the development of long-range solutions to problems such as these, Governor Edmund G. Brown appointed a Commission on Government Reform in late June, headed by the former state legislative analyst, Alan Post. The commission has a broad mandate but is confronted by the necessity to provide immediate assistance to state policymakers who will need to commence consideration of 1979-1980 fiscal matters early in 1979. Meanwhile politicians and officials in many other states — looking eagerly at the California experience for its lessons and typically not having that state's resources — face the imminent prospect of having to cope with their own homegrown tax or expenditure limitation.

Attributes and Implications of Tax and Expenditure Limits

Proposition 13 illustrates some of the characteristics and ramifications of TELs.

Over the years state governments have placed restrictions on the taxing and spending powers of local governments. Some of the more common controls that have been adopted are property tax rate (millage) limits, debt ceilings, prohibitions against certain types of taxation, and property tax levy limits. In addition, states have enacted property tax relief measures such as homestead exemptions, differential assessment ratios, and circuit breakers.

While such restraints probably held down spending and borrowing to a certain extent, they also led to governmental fragmentation and more complicated financial relationships. The effort to circumvent these traditional controls often leads to the creation of . special charges, funds, and districts and to transfers of responsibility to other levels. The newer kinds of TELs are more sophisticated and comprehensive, typically being aimed at total taxes or expenditures.

Generally, broad constraints placed on expenditures are the most manageable. While the popular protest is usually directed against high taxes, an equally strong case can be made that the real villain is the unchecked growth in spending, as legislators give in to a variety of special-interest demands. These are often implemented by state mandates that local governments perform certain functions without any provisions for added revenues. With an expenditure limit, the pressure is applied directly to the place in the budget where those interests seeking new or increased outlays have focused their efforts. With an expenditure cap, choices must be made among programs, given the maximum allowable expenditures. These can be exceeded, but only after an extraordinary vote by the legislature. Revenue limits, on the other hand, do not address directly the problem of normal growth in public demand for services, can hobble the revenue-raising system, and may lead to circumvention of the limit through greater use of charges and fees.

A critical choice is the degree of restraint. This depends primarily on how the restraint is expressed. A large variety of options are available, ranging from ratios of overall expenditures or revenues to some broad measure of economic activity, to ratios of a single revenue source to some arbitrary measure of tax base.

Most TELs attempt to curtail government expansion by setting a maximum allowable rate of growth in expenditures or taxes adjusted for rates of growth in population, price levels (inflation), or total income. In New Jersey, for example, local spending is limited by statute to a 5 percent increase over the previous year. The New Jersey expenditure limit was enacted on a three-year trial basis in 1976.

Generally formulas that are geared to the level of growth in personal income or some other measure of current economic activity permit the greatest growth in public expenditures. The specific ratios used should take into consideration the availability of data and, given the normal lag in data, the fact that today's revenues and expenditures are necessarily dependent on yesterday's performance. Hence common sense dictates that designers of limitations should allow for creation of contingency funds and reserves in cases where future conditions will not hold to past trends. By and large, TELs that express limits in terms of a general measure of total income and thus allow for growth will keep the public sector from expanding disproportionately. Yet they will avoid the arbitrariness and inequities of a restricted and sluggish measure that has little to do with overall service needs or revenue capacity.

Perhaps the most difficult TEL design problem involves the allowance for expenditure or receipts outside the overall limitation. Common provisions are for expenditures or revenues for debt-supported capital outlays or debt service to be placed outside the limit, with similar exemptions for federal grant receipts. "Emergency" expenditures and revenues to support them are also commonly exempted. On either the expenditure or revenue side of the budget, one faces the common problem of defining the degree of inclusiveness and determining what constitutes an exception. One method is to permit the limitation to be exceeded by a majority vote of the legislature. While this may appear too easy to some, it has the appeal of affixing the responsibility for increased spiraling directly to elected officials, forcing them to go on record to exceed the limit. At the same time, it retains flexibility to respond to emergencies. Abuse by elected officials of such escape clauses will lead to their removal from office or the future enactment of more onerous restrictions.

Another key feature of TELs relates to whether they are implemented at the state or local level of government or both. Clearly stringent restrictions at one level but not the other will generate forces to shift expenditure or financing responsibility to the unconstrained level. A state government operating under a TEL will undoubtedly seek fiscal relief by reducing aid payments to local governments or shifting expenditure responsibilities (perhaps with mandated levels of service) to its progeny. The appropriate design of the TEL may vary to reflect different governmental missions, resources, and data availability; therefore it seems preferable, if restraints are to be placed, to have similar limitations at both levels. However, the design of the limitations may have to differ between the levels. Local government limitations present special problems because of the multiplicity of taxing districts, the great diversity of services provided, and data limitations. Clearly the provisions of TELs should be tailored to meet the peculiar circumstances of governmental structure in each state. At a minimum, all local jurisdictions that rely on the general local tax base should be included in the restraint to minimize — if not avoid — a proliferation of special districts growing up outside the zone of governmental activity that is restricted.

A final note is the need for explicit recognition that under TELs, one level of government should not be able to transfer responsibilities to another without a specific accounting of the latter's added costs and the need for added resources. Perhaps the biggest sore point along these lines has been state governments' mandating that their local units perform certain services at specified levels without provisions for their funding. Therefore if TELs are to be equitable, they should explicitly state that such required expenditures must be funded from state sources or that the state must transfer a share of its revenue-raising capability to the local units. Similarly if functional responsibility for expenditure is shifted, then the limitations should be appropriately adjusted. For example, were the state government to absorb all welfare expenditures to the relief of local units, then the limits on both levels should be revised to reflect the greater state effort and reduced local effort that are required to maintain the equivalent level of expenditures or taxes in the aggregate.

Truth-in-Taxation Laws

A variation on the theme of TELs is the truth-in-taxation plan, also called the full disclosure tax law. This approach, which was pioneered by Florida in 1970, allows local governing bodies to set tax rates as high as they desire, provided that they follow a rigorous disclosure procedure, which includes the requirement for a public hearing on the proposed increase. Thus a full disclosure tax law is not in itself a limit on taxes or spending; instead it is a means of assuring a thorough public discussion of a proposed tax increase. Since 1970, four additional states (Hawaii, Maryland, Montana, and Virginia) and the District of Columbia have adopted truth-in-taxation laws.

Conclusion

Research to date says that tax lids and spending ceilings make a difference in states where they have been generally applied to local governments. But how such devices will operate when applied to the state itself or to both the state and local levels remains to be seen. It is also difficult to generalize about their impacts because the mechanics of TELs vary greatly. But as Proposition 13 illustrates, any TEL that comes down hard and across the board on governmental expenditures or taxes will have implications for governmental services and finances that reach far beyond next year's budget or tax bill.

Anticipation and Uncertainty

Thomas Fletcher

I don't think anyone really understands the implications of Proposition 13. I don't think we understand why it passed or what the results are going to be.

Either people have forgotten that there were two propositions on the June 6 ballot, or the fact was obscured in the smoke. One was Proposition 8; the other was Proposition 13. Proposition 8 was an effort by the state legislature to take into account what they assumed was a taxpayers' revolt. Proposition 8 cut property tax about as much as 13 did, but only on residential property; it did not cut the property tax on commercial, agricultural, and industrial property. The state legislature assumed that the voters wanted their property taxes cut but did not want expenditures cut a great deal. So the legislators put forward Proposition 8, assuming that it would certainly carry more votes than Proposition 13.

The legislature advertised the fact that if 13 passed instead of 8, a quarter of a million public employees would be laid off and public services would be substantially reduced. The legislature assumed that California voters, who have always been very wise, would see the difference between the two and would approve Proposition 8 rather than 13.

Proposition 13 got twice as many votes as 8. The purpose of Proposition 13 was not to cut taxes. It was to cut expenditures; it was to reduce the size of government, not to just cut taxes. An editorial in the *Wall Street Journal* said that any elected official who assumed that Proposition 13 meant property tax cuts would probably not be an elected official in 1979.

What happened to the 250,000 employees that were supposed to be laid off? The actual list is less than 10,000. In fact, some cities and counties are now hiring employees because they put a freeze on hiring to fill vacancies earlier. In fact the personnel cut was very small. There are two explanatory factors. One is that some cities and counties had surpluses. They had some fat, as Jarvis said they had. The second is that the state came in with a $4.1 billion bail-out. I wonder about the credibility of government in California after the advertising on the 250,000 personnel cut. People have been led to

49

believe that government is not credible. Now what must they think? Californians were told that if they voted yes on 13, services would be cut drastically. And Jarvis said, They're conning you. It's not going to happen; they won't cut those services, they won't cut those employees. And that is exactly what happened. The state did not make those cuts. How can the voters believe government the next time it tells them the consequences of Proposition 13?

We don't know the size of the cut in tax revenues on Proposition 13, because the final assessments have not yet been worked out by the county assessors. The cut is expected to be between $6 billion and $8 billion; we don't know where it will fall within that span. But we do know that the state bailed out the cities, the counties, the special districts, and the schools, in the amount of $4.1 billion.

If the public wanted the reduction of taxes, why did the state take the taxpayers' money and return it to local government? Something is wrong. I am not quite sure what is going to happen next year when the state government realizes that the public was asking to have expenditures cut. They would like to see those quarter of a million employees taken off the payroll.

One of the worst things that has happened with Proposition 13 is that the state bailed out local government. For once there was an opportunity, with good political clout, to make some adjustments in urban government services. And that political clout is gone. Now they don't have the political clout necessary to make some tough decisions that the public has been asking them to make.

With Proposition 13 property taxes can rise only 2 percent per year, substantially less than the present rate. Even more interesting is Proposition 13's provision that no new taxes can be imposed by any government agency in California unless two-thirds of those eligible to vote approve it. Note that it said those *eligible* to vote, not those voting.

In California's election system about 65 to 70 percent of the eligible voters vote in national elections. For a statewide election it's about 40 percent. For a strictly local election it's about 20 percent. There aren't even enough people voting to provide two-thirds of those eligible to vote. So the odds that any new taxation can become available to local government in California is very small.

The state had $4.1 billion of bail-out money, which was accumulated over a four-year span. This summer the state has taken a billion dollars out of next year's potential surplus by cutting income tax.

Some are saying there will be $5 billion left. Nobody knows how much surplus money, if any, there will be.

Even more important, some people are now saying that the voters wanted expenditures cut; they did not want state bail-out money. And taxes and expenditures may well be cut in the state legislature next spring.

So there is no way of knowing what the effect is going to be next year. The bail-out was for one year only.

The second unknown is the result on the economy. No one knows what is going to happen to the economy of California. About 45 to 50 percent of the tax reduction is on agricultural, commercial, and industrial property, and about half of that money leaves the state, because the headquarters are outside the state. So California stands to lose between $1.5 billion and $2 billion that would have been spent within the state. We haven't any idea of the results of that.

Even more important, we don't understand the effect on the housing industry. In California about 25 percent of the people change houses every year. But now those who buy a new house stand to pay a substantial monthly increase in cost, because the property assessment is based on its most recent selling price. This provision of Proposition 13 may well slow the housing market in California.

Those who watched the action of the state legislature and the bail-out are aware that the legislature practiced the Golden Rule. That is, he who has the gold sets the rules. And observers are aware that the state legislature, when it gave the cities, the counties, the special districts, and the schools the $4.1 billion, also handed down some restrictions. Salaries of employees were not to be raised. Police and fire services were to remain the same. And there were a number of other requirements.

Those of us who have grown up in government in California are a little astonished at the action of the legislature. A year ago the state would never have considered passing a law requiring that cities, counties, special districts not raise the pay of their employees.

Quite the contrary. The state is a collective bargaining state; they are very strong on collective bargaining; they have pushed the Myers-Millies-Brown Act. California was one of the first states to require collective bargaining. Yet this same state has said, forget the Myers-Millies-Brown Act, forget collective bargaining, forget contracts; the state is going to freeze all pay increases, if you want the state's money. It wouldn't even have been considered a year ago. Now it has been passed.

What are the strings going to be next year? We tend to look at Proposition 13 from a technical point of view, a financial, economic, taxation point of view. It is far more important to look at the governance question that Proposition 13-type philosophy is producing. Where is home rule going? We have lost home rule. A study made by the American Society for Public Administration (ASPA) this year indicates that federal government money going into thirty major cities has increased from 1 percent of their general revenue to 46 percent in just twenty years. Cities getting that much federal money are beginning to lose home rule.

The effect of the Proposition 13 concept is further erosion of home rule. I don't think the people who voted yes on 13 voted to transfer responsibility for governance to the state. I don't think it was a vote to centralize. But that is exactly what has happened. In fact, there is now more centralized government and less home rule. And I don't think the voters really intended that.

How are we going to handle this, in terms of personnel, costs, and management? I think we have to undertake an enormous amount of study and action.

I think that the stubborn mule of government, not just in California but nationally, has received the proverbial two-by-four hit on the skull. And we had better be prepared to do some following up if we don't want another blow on our thick skulls.

Ongoing Developments in California
Edward Hamilton

Perhaps the most useful thing that I can do is focus on four embry-
onic developments in California that may bear on the central issue:
What has Proposition 13 to do with anything outside a particular
period of months and a particular set of property value imbalances
and explosions within one state? It is hard to tell what message was
being sent by the electorate of California. Large numbers of political
futures rest on how one reads what happened.

There is a general sense that nobody knows quite what has been
said. Perhaps most important to understand, from the standpoint of
California and from the standpoint of the public finance structure,
is that we cannot do much competent long-term assessment, because
the event is still under way.

What we have seen so far has been just the first shock. We are
only beginning to understand its implications. The restructuring of
governmental functions, how many governments there should be,
what they ought to do, what is legitimate and illegitimate about
intergovernmental transfer, how an accountability mechanism works
in a context of massive transfers, what sorts of taxable incidents
are acceptable, whether the system is essentially visible or invisible,
whether it's progressive or flattened in terms of its income effect,
whether we're willing to live with redistribution or mechanisms
that have the effect of redistributing income in a time of considerable economic uncertainty and of relatively high inflation — these are
all issues that we are just beginning to understand.

In the last forty years our government has essentially evolved
from the layer cake model into a government where intergovernmental financial transfers, not contemplated in the Constitution,
are the dog, and the direct raising of revenues and paying for particular activities, at whatever level of government, are the tail. But
that evolution has occurred in a political context in which the main
point has been to avoid noticing that it is a lasting phenomenon.

As a result, there has not been a theoretical base, that is, a base
of intellectual infrastructure thinking, for example, about the role of
a banker government. How do the operations of a government that
is principally in the business of financing compare with those of a

government that is principally in the business of running programs? We have neither an intellectual infrastructure nor a political base for defining what government representatives do. Much of what they do is ambassadorial, that is, dealing with other levels of government, other people's tax bases, and other people's capacity to affect policy decisions.

Like the New York crisis, the California incident strikes me as an interesting event in the greening of American political theory. We now have a body politic, at least in California, that is clearly ahead of the politicians in the recognition of the growth of a marble-cake federalism, or a public sector financed from a whole series of pots without much congruence between function and revenue source.

In the debates before Proposition 13, both proponents and opponents had an unwritten but clear basic premise that nobody would mention that governments are interrelated and that state governments could no longer stand by and watch large local governments fail to produce the fundamental services that they're in business to provide.

The premise that those governments would simply close up while the states sat idly by was not plausible to the electorate. It was important only to government practitioners that this premise be maintained. The fiction of the autonomous local government is not useful to the electorate. This fiction, though not consistent with reality, has enormous uses for the practitioner, the politician, and the bureaucrat, because it provides great protections against continual raids or continual requests from other levels of government.

Most states maintain that what they do for local governments outside the simplistic formula aid programs that are concentrated primarily in education and transportation is temporary. These programs could end next week or whenever "normalcy" returns and governments can return to their layer cake independence.

California voters were saying that the layer cake world no longer exists. Most California voters could not have described the nature of the public finance system — how intergovernmental transfers occur, what kind of interplay there is between the financing levels and the operating levels of government, or who does what to whom and where the decision authority is. However, there is much evidence for a strong hunch in the electorate that the public sector is one great, gelatinous mass which, taken as a whole, has enough money to provide a reasonable level of public services. There was a hunch that if pressure is put on this mass, the resources would extrude into the vital organs so that none would do worse than others and so that all would survive.

We always attach higher wisdom to the general will of the people. Offices are won on that basis. This is one of the few examples where a reasonable case can be made for this higher wisdom. The Californian, whether or not he knew about the surplus, did not believe that the public sector would cease to operate or that large, vital services would simply cease as a result of this initiative.

The reaction to New York's crisis was born of a different set of causative factors, but the realization was the same, what might be called the greening of the federal government. When it was first suggested that the federal government might have some interest in this cataclysm, the president's response was essentially that state and city should solve their own problems. I believe that was exactly the right response at that time for dealing with the highly pressurized, internal political universe of New York. If at that moment the federal government had sought to relieve simply by saying, We are here, everybody would have rushed off to be saved by Washington. But what was really disturbing about the period 1975-1976 was that the federal government knew nothing about the internal details of state and local finance. In its entire bureaucratic structure there was nobody whose business it was to know anything about local government.

California found itself in the same situation after Proposition 13 was passed. In terms of the philosophical substructure of politics in this country, these two events dramatized the interlacing of governments. They dramatized that most people do not believe that governments are autonomous. This belief leads to a positive premise: if pressure is put on the system, governments will find some way to manage the financial distribution. Arguments based on the notion that governments are not interrelated do not succeed politically, largely because they are wrong. But the public has no positive theoretical structure for defining precisely how governments ought to be related.

Thus the question is now, What do levels and types and units of governments owe one another? The traditional answer has been nothing. It is now clear that they owe one another a great deal, but we need guidelines for handling everything from the banker government's attitude toward local government productivity to the total interface between the private money markets and government when there are many different kinds of securities issuers and debt instruments.

The events in California produced the best indication, the best laboratory demonstration, of the problem of banker government surpluses. It is a problem that we haven't had much experience with, especially since the revenues of the principal banker governments have become as volatile as they have been in the last ten years.

The short-term explanation for California's surplus was that California had experienced a 12½ percent annual average growth in per capita income for two consecutive years. That growth represents the Japanese economic miracle revisited. It is an unbelievable macroperformance, particularly given the relatively subdued recovery in the rest of the country.

The basic reason for the surpluses was that in 1971 forty-one states found themselves in the position of having to raise taxes in the trough of a recession, a politically unpleasant and not-to-be-repeated situation. They estimated the revenue yield of the tax increases in recession year terms and the tax yield came in the recovery phase. As a result, the states had a substantial reserve that allowed them to weather the 1974-1976 period, which was a deeper recession, without the enormous internal stresses that had produced general revenue sharing and a huge change in intergovernmental finance.

Thus when the 1976-1977 recovery came, these states began to reap the dividends, particularly states in the high-property-value and high-income-growth parts of the country. As a result, there were large surpluses in state and local accounts and in national income accounts.

The problem is that the United States does not have a well-defined politics of surpluses. Surpluses have generally been treated as praiseworthy. If they were criticized, it was done tongue in cheek. Criticizing surpluses was a little like criticizing a corporation for earning too high a profit or a parent for raising too healthy a child. People criticize governments for running surpluses, but the governments that were being criticized knew very well that that criticism carried with it some left-handed praise which, if allowed to circle the electorate twice, was likely to do them more good than the absence of the criticism.

We don't have a technique for thinking about, or even a tradition of thinking about, ways to deal with volatility. Countercyclical revenue sharing is the closest we've come to dealing with volatility, but we haven't really thought that through.

The enormous economic increase in California, that is, the enormous abundance with which California has been blessed the last couple of years, was essentially unpredicted. The models did not show that California would do that well. Models don't tend to be state specific and are therefore not very useful. California determines its economic base for its revenue and expenditure projections by having a conference of all the macro people involved in modeling. From that conference comes an average, because these people are usually of two camps. So some predictions are high and some are low, and the state essentially picks a midpoint and proceeds as if that midpoint were a safe projection. But, of course, a midpoint is almost always wrong.

The state doesn't want to choose either extreme. Deciding that a year is going to be a recession year or a boom year has enormous political implications, self-fulfilling prophecy problems. Therefore the state takes a middle road. If it turns out to be the wrong road, it produces massively different revenue projections, and the state suddenly has a politics-of-surplus problem.

That approach is likely to be used for some time. But some of the events since Proposition 13 was passed may give an inkling of what is likely to occur if this proposition is generalized to other states.

It was immediately clear that the surplus estimate for California's fiscal year 1979, ending June 30, 1979, was going to fluctuate during the fiscal year. It is now about $9 billion. That is the cumulative total, plus the roughly $2½ billion that will be added during the current year. There was a general feeling in the state, one of the

aspects of the politics of surplus, that the estimate ought to stabil-
ize, that it ought to be predictable in a nice, tidy way. The feeling
was that a surplus should be like a solar eclipse; one ought to be
able to predict the date and the amount and the rate without getting
fouled up in doubt and uncertainty, which is messy and leads to
unhappy client governments.

The fact is that the number is fluctuating. The state took a
moderate economic forecast, even though some models showed a
major recession in the second quarter of 1979. There are others,
including the administration, who argue that it's going to be a
relatively sober year but still show a steady economic growth pattern
at historical levels. But the quarterly numbers are suggesting a
continuation of a very large increase in personal income. As a result,
the surplus estimate is growing.

As it grows, it raises a question about the choice between tax
relief and services. This question, though not a major one, is interesting in terms of what one expects in the politics of that situation.
It is now becoming a major element, and California has voted a
billion dollars in tax relief in the last three weeks.

Many people have argued that because of the surplus the notion
of a constitutional expenditure limit, enacted by referendum, was an
unstoppable political train. In fact, a constitutional spending limit
lost in the state legislature three weeks ago on the assembly side by
a large number of votes. Every one of those votes against and for
was cast by somebody who was running in November. The entire
California state legislature runs in November, with the exception
of any Republican member of the state senate who is returning,
which is an interesting political phenomenon when one is trying
to negotiate a package.

The point is that it is not open season for all kinds of financial
limitations, all kinds of flat constitutional, long-term bars against
public spending. Even in California it's not, and it seems very unlikely that it will be in other states in some direct, cause-and-effect
relation that many people like to predict.

The interesting evolution to watch in California is the constant
interplay between those who believe the problem is the way the
money is raised and those who believe that the problem is how much
money is raised. What has happened in California has been clearly
a stopgap measure. It has not been a long-term response.

A measure such as Proposition 13 produces a situation in which a long-term response cannot be formulated in a sensible way and immediately put into effect. In California the effect of Proposition 13 was particularly painful because the election came on June 6 and the fiscal year for all sixty-five hundred entities in the state ended twenty-four days later. All those entities by law had to budget for the entire fiscal year; they could not budget for parts of the coming fiscal year.

They also faced requirements concerning unemployment benefits. Under the expiring unemployment insurance law, employees had to be laid off by the first of August or the federal government would not pay three-quarters of the unemployment benefits. Of course, this provision would have doubled the financial requirements for layoffs, because the state would have to finance whatever unemployment benefits were to be provided.

The stopgap mechanism is a straight banker revenue-sharing distribution program, which is not adequate. Technically it is simplistic in many respects. We were trying to evolve the formulas that were the least silly in terms of their effects. The problem was to allocate $9 billion on a given Thursday in June, using only those general distribution formulas that have existed between the state and its various programmatic agencies. In California all programs are categorical. There's very little support from the general budget, except for the school districts. But, if those formulas are used as a model, because they are politically familiar and therefore passable, then mistakes will be cemented. Those mistakes are inversely proportional to information. That is, the state knew much about school districts and almost as much about counties, at least, the health and welfare aspects of county budgets. The state knew much less about the cities and nothing about the forty-seven hundred special districts, the entities that most distinguish California's government from that of other states.

In the bail-out program the level of precise allocation principle and reasonably equitable and responsive provision of aid is directly proportional to position on this scale. The more the state knew about a given level of government the better the job the state could do in determining the formula criteria by which money was distributed to that class of government or activity.

That approach is difficult to correct. The bail-out program was hardest on the special districts. These districts range from mosquito abatement districts to major hospitals and transit districts. Their dependence on the property tax ranges from 100 percent in the case of fire districts, for example, to a couple of percent in the case of some hospitals and transit operations.

There was not enough time or information in that period to devise a formula that was sensitive to those differences. Yet the legislature would not enact a statute that would have corrected the inequities for those formulas, for the same reason. We still don't have a data base that allows the legislature to know what it is doing when it enacts across-the-board principles in the special district category.

The restructuring of California's public finance is now in the hands of the Post Commission. Restructuring was the second step of the two-step strategy of the bail-out bill. The first step is the distribution of surplus funds, which continues for two years in order not to build a precipice into the transition period. The other side of that transition — doing something about jurisdictions, inter-governmental finances, and functional distributions — is the re-sponsibility of the nine-member commission chaired by Alan Post, the retired chief of California's Legislative Analysis Unit. That's where the activity is now going on.

They are locked in internal combat about whether to take a near-term look or whether to consider a massive restructuring. The latter choice would mean that the group has to stay in business for two or three years. It's a very uneasy group. Two of its members are Ronald Reagan's finance director and the chief of the state AFL-CIO. The commission may not be a feasible long-term vehicle because its own internal mechanics, chemistry, may not work well.

Meanwhile, of course, other political actors are trying to be-come the parents of the long-term public finance structure of Cali-fornia. That battle is likely to continue each legislative session for the next four to six sessions, before the outlines of the response are drawn.

Most people agree that the present situation is not tolerable over the long term and that the formulas, which are usually built on one to three years of experience, have too many distortions and expect the history to remain static. Most people therefore agree that something major has to be done. Thus the development to watch, if one is talking about what will happen in California, is what the thinking process produces at what periods, and what political configuration greets that emergence. What will emerge from the conflicting forces?

To make such a prediction nationally, therefore, one must be able to predict both the evolution of that kind of sequence in the states that decide to move in this direction and the federal response. The central point is that there is a philosophical and practical leaning to broader and broader tax bases to finance all levels of government services. This results primarily from people's mobility and our tendency to be as messy as possible about the distribution of power in metropolitan areas. At the same time there is a fairly strong and continuing sense, philosophical and otherwise, that we want expenditure decisions to be made by a smaller and narrower group. We want the decision to be made at the local level and the district level and the neighborhood level. We want people to be able to affect their own lives. We want government that we can understand and feel close to and trust. That tends to be local government. But we want that government financed by something that is farther away and therefore has more purchase on the tax base.

California is in the immediate aftershock. It has managed to maintain public services because its peculiar public finance structure has produced a large surplus. California is thinking about the longer-term problems to which Proposition 13 requires answers but to which it provides no useful answers.

Additional Comment by Edward Hamilton

Proposition 13 provides interesting commentary on the planning process, on crisis planning. That is, what can a government, particularly a banker government, do to prepare itself for a likely change?

Three aspects of the question need to be considered. First, the likelihood of passage of Proposition 13 really mushroomed only about forty-five to sixty days before the election.

In almost every election California has any number of propositions on the ballot. Two things usually happen. One, propositions regarded by the movers and shakers in the state as nonsense usually do not pass. Two, any proposition that does pass usually doesn't make it through the courts. Of the seven initiatives that have passed in the last ten years, five have been thrown out by the courts.

The point is that the expected in California didn't happen, particularly when the legislature, after having labored for a year and a half, came out with Proposition 8. Virtually every politician in the state started campaigning for Proposition 8. Then assessment notices for the coming year appeared. The average home owner in Los Angeles found his assessment rising by 85 percent. In a single year that great an increase causes enormous problems unless the tax rate is dropped, and there was no prospect that the rate would be dropped enough to give real relief.

Second, work was enormously affected before the election by the prospect that the work itself might affect the outcome of the election. The work of projecting budgets and anticipating programmatic changes that would occur if the proposition passed were all made in the light of the fact that the projection itself could help defeat the proposition. As a result, the work was almost useless for figuring out what was to be done the morning after if the proposition passed.

The first year of a massive reduction is not a typical year; it is a very atypical year. So predictions of what is going to happen in the first year, not an average year, must take all kinds of complexities into account. Politicians believe, and with good reason, that people are impatient with the need to consider these complexities.

But predicting what will happen in the first year after a government has received an enormous revenue reduction, for example, requires answers to these questions: Does the government have any reserves? (Answer: Some yes, some no.) What is the fringe cost of layoffs? That is, how much severance pay and various kinds of benefits must be paid? In the first year the number of people who have to be laid off is always larger than the average for the first five years to reach a given expenditure cut because there are extra payments required as part of severance expenses. As a result, the long-term prediction is not what will happen in the first year. None of the predictions of exactly what would occur if the proposition passed had much utility, with one exception, the shadow budget of Los Angeles County, the largest county in the state and the second largest municipal service provider in the country.

Third, the politicians involved had a very serious problem. They felt that letting anyone know that contingency planning on a major scale was going on might make the political difference. The governor has been criticized for revealing, ten days before the proposition was passed, that contingency planning was going on. He was criticized by opponents of the proposition on the ground that he had given up hope for its defeat. That kind of political negative on contingency planning is a real problem.

There probably weren't five members of either house who had given serious thought to the precise sequence of decisions that would be necessary and the options that would be open in the course of making those decisions if this proposition passed. And the question was whether it would be possible without such planning to take the necessary action in three weeks.

We did in fact produce the action, and I'm happy to defend it in detail. I believe it was the best possible and on the whole substantially better than I thought it would be. Yet one of the reasons for its existence may be the lack of contingency planning. If each member had been doing serious simulation, if we had not been in shock, if everybody had felt secure in his own notion of what should occur, then I'm not sure that it could have been produced so quickly. So there is an interesting theoretical issue of whether something can be done any better than it was done.

Proposition 13 and the Financing of Public Services
John J. Kirlin

The Jarvis-Gann initiative, approved by California voters on June 6, 1978, dramatically affects the financing of public services in that state. Property tax revenues to local governments were reduced $7 billion, approximately a 60 percent reduction of total property tax revenues and a 22 percent cut in total local government expenditures in California. The state legislature allocated the remaining $4.4 billion of property taxes on a pro rata basis among local governments. This amount was allocated from the county level to cities, county, and special districts according to the average percentage of all property taxes collected, exclusive of taxes levied for debt retirement, over the past three fiscal years, while the pro rata distribution to school districts was based only on their FY1977-1978 property tax revenues.

Drawing on an existing state surplus of approximately $5.5 billion, the state also distributed "state assistance for property tax loss" on a one-year basis as follows:

Cities. Apportionment based on each city's property tax loss relative to all cities statewide $250 million

Counties. (a) State assumption of various mandated health and welfare programs

Medi-Cal	$418 million
SSI/SSP	168 million
AFDC	437 million
Food Stamp Administration	21 million
	$1,044 million
(b) Block grant to counties	$ 436 million
Total to counties	$1,480 million

Special districts.

    (a) Apportioned to counties on the basis of that county's special districts collective property tax loss in relation to statewide special district proper-

> ty tax loss, to be allocated among its special
> districts by each county $ 125 million

(b) An "unmet needs" reserve for special districts
is to be allocated by the State Department of
Finance $ 37 million

Public schools (K-12). An additional block grant is made, based
on a sliding scale that provides low-spending schools with approximately 91 percent of their 1978-1979 budgets and high-
spending districts a maximum of 85 percent of their budgets
$2,000 million

County offices of education	65 million
Community colleges	240 million
Total state assistance	$4,197 million

In addition, the state established a $900 million emergency loan
fund, designed to alleviate distress caused by any loss of access to
the commercial market for revenue and tax anticipation notes and
to avoid possible defaults on such existing instruments as tax allocation and lease-purchase bonds.

Predictably this state assistance also included various restrictions.
Most notable are prohibition of any cost-of-living salary increases
for employees of local governments receiving assistance, prohibition of any AFDC cost-of-living increase, and requirements that
police and fire services be given highest priority in city and county
budgets so that these service levels are maintained at FY1977-1978
levels.

New Demands on the Intergovernmental System

The one-year bail-out of local government using the state surplus
is only a temporary palliative to Proposition 13's ultimate effects.
New state action will be needed next year, quite likely in the context
of a smaller surplus. The impacts on federal programs are only now
being catalogued, and pressures for adjustments in federal policies
and programs will surely increase. Local governments have fore-
stalled sizable firings of employees, but FY1978-1979 local government budgets are commonly reduced 10 to 15 percent from pre-

Proposition 13 projections, and some jurisdictions (especially special districts that rely on property taxes) have suffered more substantial reductions. The eventual loss of three hundred thousand jobs in the public sector is still anticipated. Attitude surveys of citizens show continued support for Proposition 13, but clientele are unhappy with cuts in some services.

It should come as no surprise that Proposition 13, directed at property taxes imposed by local governments, immediately reverberated effects throughout the intergovernmental system. Nevertheless it is apparent that citizens, public employees, and policymakers are not well prepared for the impacts of Proposition 13 on the intergovernmental system. Three examples illustrate the deficiencies in our appreciation of the existing interdependencies that were increased by Proposition 13.

First, while it is erroneous to attribute Proposition 13 votes to any deep dissatisfaction with public services, it is clear that if cuts are to be made, citizens nominate welfare programs as their first priority for reductions. Yet this service is only minimally controllable by local governments, because most funding comes from federal and state sources and service delivery is tightly circumscribed by federal and state regulations. Not only will Proposition 13 lead to cuts in services most supported by citizens, it will also enfeeble local government, the jurisdictional level that citizens consistently evaluate more favorably than state and federal levels.

Second, public employees were shocked when the state legislature prohibited any cost-of-living salary increases for local government employees and removed such increases from the state budget. Even if litigation successfully challenges this action in cases where it abrogated existing collective bargaining agreements, it is clear that the state can effectively determine future salary levels of local government employees.

Third, state policymakers discovered that they did not possess adequate information about local governments to make effective policies. Information was adequate only for functions such as education, health and welfare for which the state already had extensive service delivery partnerships with local governments. For other functions, and for cities and special districts generally, ignorance and misinformation plagued policymaking. For example, state allocations

for special districts did not even meet the requirements of fire protection special districts which were to receive sufficient funds to
continue 1977-1978 service levels before allocations were made to
other special districts. Federal policymakers, after an initial period of
disregarding Proposition 13's effects on their programs, are now
realizing that the impacts are likely to be substantial and that they
also lack information on which to develop policy adjustments.

Among the many intergovernmental dilemmas posed by Proposition 13, the following are among the most perplexing.

1. *How may the total size of the public sector be least harm-
fully reduced?* Obviously at stake here are the premise that replacement revenues will not be found for the lost property taxes and the
possible ambiguity and difference of opinion concerning the definition of harmful effects. Nationwide attitude surveys and politicians'
actions strongly suggest that pressure to reduce the size of the public sector is a potent political movement. Next year may see a new
issue, but policies made under these pressures will likely continue
to have an effect. The finances and the service delivery systems of
local, state, and federal governments are so intertwined that reduction of the fiscal resources available to one set of jurisdictions
causes strain and readjustment throughout the intergovernmental
system. Thus when the public sector is reduced, the total system
must be rebalanced. This articulation is difficult not only because
there are numerous separate decision points, but also because various
decision makers face differing constraints and opportunities. These
differences are *horizontal* (cities differ from counties and from
states), *vertical* (differing service delivery systems exhibit fundamentally different degrees of integration and interdependence;
for example, the welfare system is more integrated and interdependent than the "policing" system), and *particularistic* (jurisdictions
have differential access to resources and different political forces
acting as constraints).

Among the "harmful" possibilities inherent in such an interdependent system, two are most common. The first is that components of interdependent systems become unbalanced; one element
of the system changes in ways that are not matched by others. An
example is the justice system, where police, courts, and corrections
systems ideally have similar capacities to process those accused of

breaking the law, but different decision makers control each element. The second possibility is that the decisions needed to adjust service levels for a particular service simply are not made at some decision points so that paralysis results. This is most likely in cases where service delivery is a local responsibility but most funding decisions and the crucial decisions concerning how services are to be rendered are made by the state and federal governments. Health, education, and welfare services are examples. Yet another possible harmful outcome would be overcentralization of policymaking spurred by a desire to overcome the previous two possibilities, which would debilitate the decentralized decision-making abilities that characterize the present intergovernmental system and often lead to better service delivery as desirable variations emerge.

2. *How may the federal and state governments responsibly perform their enhanced "banker" roles?* As Edward K. Hamilton has observed, the federal and state governments are emerging as bankers who raise revenues and then disburse them to local governments for actual service provision. Proposition 13 accelerates this trend, reducing the present and future capacity of California local governments to generate their own revenues. The similar measures being considered in other states also usually constrain local government most tightly, although some also constrain the state. Unless states and the federal government also become constrained by revenue limits, they will experience increasing pressure to further bankroll local governments.

Even with adequate resources, the dilemmas of performing the banker role are substantial. Because the revenues of state and federal governments fluctuate with the condition of the economy, they must steer a careful course between revenue shortfall and politically embarrassing surplus. The federal government may manage these fluctuations through borrowing; states cannot, because they do not have the ability to run deficit budgets. Another problem is that superior levels of government never have adequate information for good policymaking concerning local governments. As a consequence they almost invariably seek to reduce the number of jurisdictions they must deal with, mandate procedures, and audit performance. In short, they seek to make governments conform to a hierarchical, bureaucratic model. These efforts lead to the same dysfunctions that analysts of bureaucratic organizations have recognized for decades: rigidity, substitution of rule compliance for performance, and inability to learn. Alternative policy strategies are needed, and because habit and intellect are so ingrained with administrative control approaches, even identifying alternatives is not an easy task.

3. *How may weaker or general interests be protected from stronger interest groups?* Movement of decision-making powers from local governments to the state and federal levels may well give an advantage to stronger interest groups, which have the capacity to offer campaign support to legislators and to maintain representatives in state and federal capitols. On the other hand, widely dispersed interests may be better able to organize at a higher level of aggregation than was possible when decisions affecting their interest were widely dispersed. Regardless of the ultimate strengthening and weakening of particular interests, it is certain that the structure of interest representation will change to reflect the new distribution of political power and that changed decision rules will emerge.

Particularly perplexing is how state and federal legislators should respond to representatives of local governments. These public interest groups or state and local interest groups (PIG's or SLIG's as they are called at the federal level) differ from other interest groups in two crucial ways: they can offer no campaign support, and they consist of representatives presumably advancing the interests of the citizens who elected them. They are different from a brewers' association, Teamsters' union, or realtors' association, yet legislatures attuned to interest groups do not easily accommodate the difference.

Much of this difficulty in establishing a role for representatives of subordinate governments results from the tensions between homogeneity and particularism in policymaking. If policies are presumed to be ideally homogeneous, applying uniformly and unambiguously in all situations, then no special standing need be given representatives of locales. If policies are not to be homogeneous, or if they cannot be applied uniformly and unambiguously, then representatives of locales have an enhanced, crucial, and legitimate role in assisting in the development of policy that strikes the appropriate balance between homogeneity and particularism. It is my impression that more inclusive governments experience great pressure to make homogeneous policies, largely on the grounds of equity and simplicity, and often err in that direction, seeking homogeneous policies where particularism may be desirable along with more flexibility among localities.

To conclude, Proposition 13 greatly affects the financing of public services. It is unlikely that sufficient waste exists to allow continuation of existing services with such reduced revenues. In its bail-out legislation the state of California constrained the ability of local governments to search for economies by stipulating that police and fire services were to be maintained at the existing level. Proposition 13 enfeebles local government, reducing its ability to generate its own revenues. Because government is better characterized as an intergovernmental system rather than as autonomous units, with intertwined fiscal and service delivery systems, a reduction of local revenues of the magnitude caused by the Jarvis-Gann initiative immediately reverberates at the state and federal levels. Adjusting to these changes in the intergovernmental system is among the most critical and perplexing requirements of the post-Proposition 13 era.

Part Three
Outlook for Localities
and Improved Management

Tax Restrictions: A Public Administrator's View

Keith F. Mulrooney

Proposition 13 and its aftermath have formed one of the leading public administration events of the decade, if not the whole post-World War II period. I have four observations, seven predictions, and three comments on the implications of Proposition 13.

My first observation: The cities, counties, schools, and special districts of California have suffered a loss of power under Proposition 13 and will continue to do so.

Second, the penalizing of the financial powers of cities and counties as a result of alleged fiscal abuses has occurred before in American history and is likely to occur again. It occurred after the municipal railroad bond issue defaults of the 1870s and 1880s and some of the land speculation in the early 1900s. Decades were required to liberalize some of the worst restrictions laid on local government's financing powers. In many cases they were never removed. We ought to think about that now as such restrictions are again being imposed on local governments.

Third, the future is not really too far away. We shall soon find out just how contagious this California disease is in the rest of the country, in state and local government and in the nation.

Fourth, Proposition 13 has already badly hurt, perhaps fatally, the tax increment method of redevelopment financing that is widely used in California.

My first prediction: Cities will survive.

Second, although the conditions are not the same in other states, the Proposition 13 fever is most likely to spread in various ways at least to some other states and to some other countries, particularly Canada.

Third, management's hand in bargaining with local government employee unions will be strengthened.

Fourth, minority employment gains of recent years will suffer, but the extent depends substantially on the abruptness of the phase-in period for Proposition 13. Los Angeles County has hired only 39 percent of its white employees but 63 percent of its black, 83 percent of its Hispanics, and 84 percent of its Asian Pacific group during the past ten years.

The $5 billion bailout this first year has eased the situation substantially. It looks as if there could be more than a $4 billion surplus in the second year. Applying it as a bailout again will help reduce minority displacement in hiring.

Fifth, limits on taxes and spending will bring about a certain amount of structural reform or at least structural change in government, with a shift of certain functions, particularly welfare, to higher levels of government.

In California the combined effect of the Serrano decision and Proposition 13 is a radical upward shift in the percentage of school board budgets supplied by the state and a corresponding decrease in the percentage supplied from local resources. In one school district in California in just one year, the percentage of the school board budget raised from local revenue sources has gone down from 7 percent in the fiscal year just concluded to 4 percent in this current fiscal year.

That reduction is linked with the amazing shift that has occurred in the last twenty years in funding by higher-level government, the banker role of government. The Advisory Commission on Intergovernmental Relations has noted that the federal share of the city budget of fifteen large cities has increased from 1.1 percent to 47.5 percent between 1957 and 1978, a twenty-year period.

Sixth, wherever the tax rollbacks go into effect, some additional private sector investment should emerge, but we are not able to predict exactly what that is yet. Fortunately, there are studies going on in California, of just what that effect is.

Seventh, strong efforts will be made to place similar restrictions on federal taxation, and they will fail. There may be a period of conservative cutbacks in federal spending, but actual fixed limitations, I predict, will fail.

As to my comments: Some observers, particularly the optimists, say that we will now be able to make the changes in government that we always wanted to make but never seemed able to do.

Whether such changes would require constitutional amendments or state legislative changes remains to be seen. Outside the Portland area there is no strong evidence that the voters are any more eager for regional government now, for example, than they were before voting on Proposition 13.

The results and recommendations of the Post Commission in California will be very interesting with regard to restructuring and reallocating of functions.

Second, the universities may have to change their training programs or at least the emphasis of those programs, stressing hard-nosed budgeting, productivity improvements and even more juggling of the intergovernmental system than we have seen in the recent past.

The universities in California are already starting to see the effects from Proposition 13. The public administration programs are becoming victims to a certain extent; since fewer governments are able to give tuition reimbursement to their employees, so fewer employees are enrolling in graduate programs in public administration, and some undergraduate students are now questioning whether they should seek a career in public administration.

Third, I think we are going to see a premature halt, at least in California, to the growing movement of the last ten years of cities into the social sector. I hate to see that, because I think it was one of the more promising trends in California and nationally.

Whatever we do, we had better get on with it. Hand wringing will do no good. The situation calls for strong leadership and good public management.

Proposition 13 and Its Consequences for Public Management
Richard J. Davis

California's adoption of Proposition 13 was to be sure an important event. It was not, however, as it has been frequently characterized, a turning point in public concern about government spending. Efforts to close the ever-widening revenue-expenditure gap are not new. During the seventies local governments have faced a slowdown in the growth rate of federal government assistance, double-digit inflation, and a recession worse than any since the Great Depression. The financial difficulties of New York City, Yonkers, Cleveland, and other communities are indicative of the serious problems facing local government. Local schools have been unable to open on time or have had to close early because of inadequate funds and an unwillingness of the public or their elected representatives to provide sufficient funds to support local education programs on a full-time basis. The success of local governments in obtaining public approval of local bond issues has deteriorated sharply in recent years.

/ Proposition 13 does not represent something new. But it is not simply a property tax revolt. It is an extreme and exaggerated example of difficulties that local governments have been facing for many years. The special circumstances in California — rapidly rising tax assessments and a $5 billion state surplus with no plans for its use — helped create the extreme reactions of California's citizens/ Other states adopted, before Proposition 13, devices for limiting the growth of state expenditures. Still other states have considered similar proposals, and many are considering them now. Perhaps more important, mayors, city councils, and the public through the political process have been severely restricting the ability of local government to finance additional activities and in some cases have made it necessary to significantly reduce local public spending and services.

Proposition 13 does not seem to be the real issue. The real issue is, What does Proposition 13 symbolize? What is it an example of? Is it a taxpayer revolt? Is it a quest for property tax reform? Is it an expression of a lack of confidence in government? Is it an expression of public frustration with high inflation and a slow-growing economy which have resulted in a loss of real income for many? Does it represent the public's desire for greater fiscal accountability? Perhaps all these factors are at the root of the growing public resistance to higher taxes and higher levels of government spending unless they have a clear understanding and appreciation of how much they are getting for their money.

Staff at the Conference of Mayors coined the phrase *political management,* which embraces the increasing attention that mayors are giving to political decision making about management issues. Management and finance now receive more attention in local elections than they have received in the past. The questions which taxes to cut or to raise, what function should be carried out by local government, which services should be cut require a combination of political and managerial decision making. Mayors and city councils are increasingly being held accountable for their ability to make wise political management decisions. Thus the economic and social problems of the seventies have led to increasing involvement of political leadership in managerial questions at the local level.

A second development stemming from the circumstances of the seventies has been the growing importance of the strategic use of public funds and authorities to achieve public goals through private action. In Portsmouth, Virginia, we developed a project in which the private sector built a public building for the city's use. This arrangement typifies the attempt by an increasing number of localities to use public powers to influence private investment in ways that are profitable for the private sector and at the same time achieve public goals.

The high priority given to improved management of local government is a third result of the experience of the seventies. Many elected officials are now viewing city government as a corporation, much as a private free-enterprise corporation president attempts to deal with making a profit. Productivity is not simply a buzz word for local officials; it means specific measures to get a more efficient operation, to find and promote employees based on their performance, to identify measures by which city government activities can be evaluated and monitored. Labor management relations is another critical area for elected officials. In some cities productivity measures are being made a part of collective bargaining agreements. Several mayors have resisted what they felt were budget-busting labor union agreements and have had to withstand recall petitions in order to maintain the fiscal integrity of their city government.

This private-corporation approach to the management of local government has many hazards. However, most mayors recognize the need for a political balance between the needs of the citizens and the maintenance of the city's fiscal integrity. The real test for the elected official is whether the public is satisfied with the management. Simply balancing the books is not enough. The manner in which the books are balanced and what receives priority must be subjected to the scrutiny of the voters through the ballot box. Thus it is impossible to look at local government exclusively as a private corporation. It is more difficult to achieve an efficient, well-managed, fiscally sound local government than to make a profit in the private business world.

A final hoped-for consequence of Proposition 13 was addressed in some detail in a resolution adopted at the Annual Meeting of the Conference of Mayors. The title of that resolution, "Tax Reform and Needed Municipal Services," is indicative of its content. The issue of tax reform and local needs has been the subject of discussion for many years at U.S. Conference of Mayors meetings. We hope that the Proposition 13 fever will encourage a nationwide debate about the need for altering the intergovernmental fiscal system. Many organizations such as the Advisory Commission on Intergovernmental Relations have made proposals to overhaul it. Other studies have been made to determine which level of government should most appropriately provide certain public services and which levels of government should collect taxes to pay for those government services. Some items should be paid for and administered at the local level. Other governmental functions should be administered at the local level but financed by federal taxes. The present crazy-quilt system should be changed. It will take a long time to do it but the time to start is now. The Conference of Mayors has supported proposals for a national health insurance, for reform of the welfare system, and for a shifting of the burden of financing educational services. Many of these proposals would require a major shifting of responsibilities within the intergovernmental system. These are what we believe should be the consequences of the Proposition 13 debate and discussion.

A Poorman's Guide to Restricting Local Government Taxes

Elisha C. Freedman

Three and a half years ago I closed a deal on an interagency grant with the National Science Foundation, the Department of Energy, the Department of Commerce's Economic Development Administration, and the Department of Housing and Urban Development. It has been one of the best-kept secrets in Washington.

The grant provided money to test some new technology for digging tunnels deeper and faster. Rochester was able, with federal help, to dig a tunnel from Lake Ontario forty miles due south to the Finger Lakes town of Naples, New York, the home of Widmer Wine Company. The tunnel was wide enough to run two ten-wheelers side by side. Unfortunately the project came to a dead end at the north wall of the Widmer wine cellar. The men working on the project haven't been seen since, and the grant expired after Rochester agreed to fill in the hole.

The objective of this mission was to extend the tunnel to North Carolina and then move the city of Rochester through it. It would have been a monumental feat of urban technology, accomplishing what no other city has been able to do — namely, do what industries and citizens have been doing steadily for the past fifteen years, leave the Northeast for the South and a new start.

The message of this silly tale is that municipal government cannot pull up stakes, cut taxes, and start over in a new place. It has to make the best of the situation where it is.

For those toiling in the big cities of New York State, making the best of the situation these days generally refers to handling New York's older and less-publicized version of Proposition 13. This paper describes the New York approach to restricting property taxation and how one local government and the state legislature dealt with it. If the trend toward state restrictions on local taxation and spending continues and intensifies, then major changes in the way state and federal governments interact with one another and with local governments will be necessary; political styles and citizen expectations must adjust accordingly; and both public employees and management will have to be more productive.

There are three major positions that one can take on Proposition 13. At one extreme is the emotional throw-the-baby-out-with-the-bathwater approach characteristic of the Jarvis-Gann movement. Applied in a state without California's huge surplus, that approach would be a dangerous gamble. At the other end of the spectrum is the turn-back-the-clock group who believe that the Proposition 13 movement can be beaten on the basis of logic and a sense of social responsibility. In the middle are those who recognize that Proposition 13 represents a spirit of government reform and an opportunity to bring about creative and constructive responses to the demands for more equitable taxing systems and the elimination of waste in government. These people believe in looking at both sides of the fiscal picture — income and expenditures — and oppose a compulsive, rigid solution to a complex and nonuniform problem.

My paper takes the middle ground but cautions that the middle-ground position may be meaningless unless there is organization and leadership behind it. It suggests the middle ground as a prominent feature of a national urban policy.

Many states have had restrictions on local expenditure or tax-raising abilities for some time. I have always opposed restrictions by state governments over the power of local officials to meet local needs as interfering with home rule. However, my experience has convinced me that there must be some control or limitation over the extent of discretion that can be exercised by local officials.

In one city where I worked there were no controls over local spending and collective bargaining abuses took place. I used to attribute the interference of mayor and councilmen in negotiations to unfamiliarity with a new and complicated governmental process. In reality they had been bought by the municipal unions and were paying off their debts or buying new support. No ballot box could work effectively in that city, since it was overwhelmingly a one-party community.

In contrast, the city that I am currently serving has been operating under a New York State constitutional provision that limits the amount of money it can raise from the property tax for current expenses (everything but debt or capital outlay) to 2 percent of the current value of taxable real property in the community. I contend that this restriction has been a primary factor in promoting fiscal prudence and that without it there would be less incentive to economize and explore new approaches to providing more efficient and economical services.

However, such taxing limitations also have the reverse effect. When the limitation allows considerable spending leeway, the tendency is to be carefree until close to the margin. When the margin is close, as it was in Rochester when I was hired in January 1974, there is a clear incentive to merge good management with the goals of good politics and to focus on a common enemy — lurking municipal bankruptcy.

Lack of Rationality of New York State's Tax-Limit Policy

New York State's approach to controlling local use of the property tax varies considerably from the approaches of states that impose millage limits for all expenditures and varies from those that permit local referenda to exceed such limits.

By excluding debt services and capital expenditures from this policy, New York's constitution indirectly encourages localities to play games with borrowing and to hide operational costs in their bonded expenditure programs to get around the property tax limits. Unlike Proposition 13, New York's constitution does not treat all its local jurisdictions alike. Rochester is limited to 2 percent for both city and school operations, while cities with a population below 125,000 have a 2 percent limit on municipal operations plus a limit of 1¼ percent to 2 percent on schools. Counties have different controls; and towns, some of which are as large or larger than Rochester, have no restrictions.

There is no reason for the varied restrictions. For instance when Albany's population dropped below 125,000, its spending limit increased from 2 percent for both city and schools, as in the case of Rochester, to 2 percent for municipal functions and 1½ percent for education, a total of 3½ percent. In other words, New York logic implies that a smaller population means greater ability to raise funds through property taxation.

Legislative Attempts to Circumvent Tax Limits

In carrying out this philosophy of government the state legislature has several times come to the rescue of Rochester and other jurisdictions having trouble with their constitutional limits. Its most noteworthy rescue effort was to pass a law that overruled the constitutional taxing limits so that pension and social security costs could be paid.

In a 1974 taxpayer suit the courts ruled this law invalid. Undaunted, the legislature passed another law to get around the constitution and even included in the law a section that would become effective if the new law was also ruled unconstitutional. That section would have permitted raising a state property tax (in lieu of a local one) which then would be distributed to each locality that had exceeded its tax limit. This law was also ruled unconstitutional. The initial effect was to be a reduction of 32.1 percent in property taxes and a $32 million cutback in operating expenses.

The court decision came almost at the moment the 1978-1979 budget was to be submitted. Dealing with the problem required a delicate orchestration of local decision making and supportive action from the state legislature and the county government. What made the problem even more difficult was that during the previous four years Rochester had cut seven hundred full-time positions, or 17.5 percent of an original four thousand full-time positions. There was little left to cut without clearly reducing services. The city had begun a revitalization effort to stay competitive with the suburban ring of towns, any one of which would have been over the 2 percent limit if it had had one. To continue this effort, the city council would have had to persuade the state legislature to authorize alternative revenues in conjunction with the necessary service cuts.

As might be expected, there were varied opinions about what should be done. Natural fears of political loss and unacceptable metropolitan solutions were mixed with the conviction that the city's problems were due to its reliance on questionable laws passed by the state legislature. There was strong feeling that it was the legislature's responsibility to resolve these problems and that any attempt by the city to devise solutions before the legislature did would only reduce the incentive for the legislature to act.

The state legislature did find a solution, not at all the way that California's legislature did, but by devising a fiscal gimmick. It merely redefined how current property value would be determined to provide a more current and thus higher base to calculate the expenditure limitations. This solution cost the state nothing, and it reduced the combined overage of the Rochester city government and school district by $7.2 million, from $32 million to $24.8 million. It also took care of the problems of nearly all the sixty-two small city school districts that were in trouble, thereby lessening the legislature's interest in Rochester and the big upstate cities.

The state legislature also found a way to resolve the remaining $24.8 million problem in typical New York style. It set up a loan fund. Legislators told local officials and municipal union leaders not to worry about paying back the loans, that they would be forgiven. This tactic was a real case of legislative loansharking, designed to put the borrowers into a deeper hole the following year. It is no wonder that New York City has had a debt problem, considering this prevailing philosophy of municipal finance. Rochester, having already been stung by previous legislative rescue attempts, refused to accept the loan concept.

Seeing that the state legislature would not come up with the cash, the city council reluctantly asked it for authorization to charge for waste collection service, levy special assessments for street lighting, increase the utilities' gross receipts tax, and legalize an approach to a metro police force.

The majority of the local state legislators voted no on the city proposals, none of which required state money. They feared retribution in the fall elections. However, all but the metro police bill went forward (and that because it needed more work and would not have mitigated the city's immediate fiscal crisis). The rest were passed thanks to legislators from other parts of the state who could vote presumably without fear of ballot-box retaliation. But there was a catch. A two-year sunset provision was included; at the end of two years the new revenue-producing measures will die unless renewed. It was generally implied that some new, less painful alternatives would be discovered within the two years.

There has been no revaluation of city property since 1937 and that valuation was based on prices during the period 1926-1930; thus the great majority of homes in Rochester carry assessments in the $3000-$5000 range. Industry and utilities have borne the major portion of the property tax and have essentially subsidized many of the services received by the small home owner. Taking waste collection and street lighting from the property tax and including them as separate charges on the tax bill would increase the burden on the small taxpayer while reducing it for the so-called fat cats. Likewise, raising the utilities' gross receipts tax would be reflected, in part, on the monthly utility bills, again a potential political no-no even though tax-exempt organizations would pick up part of the burden.

In the end the council closed the remaining $24.8 million gap by using the new revenues for $9.5 million, cutting programs by $10.5 million, and making up the balance through fund transfers and adjustments. In all, three hundred city and school district positions were eliminated. It was abundantly clear that the legislators' fiscal gimmick extending the tax margin by $7.2 million made the difference between squeeze and strangulation. Although property taxes were cut by 24.6 percent, the actual reduction in payments to the city and the school board for the fictional average taxpayer in Rochester with the $5000 assessment and forty-foot frontage amounted to $43.72.

However, closing that gap did not close the book on this fiscal year. New York State has compulsory binding arbitration for policemen and firemen. State arbitrators have the legal power to set salaries, and the funds for these salaries must be provided by the local jurisdiction, in this case a jurisdiction that cut money for proposed wage settlements from the budget to meet the tax limit. What happens when the city has reached its taxing limit, has a shrinking tax base, and cannot raise the additional money? What should be cut to meet the arbitration decision? It will be interesting to see what happens when two state mandates — the constitutional property tax restriction and statutory compulsory binding arbitration — collide head-on.

What I am describing begins to look like a Keystone Cops comedy, with mobs of actors tripping and falling over one another while the suspect gets away. The federal level pumps in millions of dollars in community development, general revenue sharing, CETA, education, transportation, and other aid to keep the city going and competitive. At the same time the interactions of state mandates reduce the levels of important services such as police, fire, and education, generally associated with helping to retain people in the city.

Add to this situation the indecisiveness at the state capitol when it comes to determining fiscally prudent alternatives, and the continued municipal pressure on Washington for still more financial assistance becomes understandable. It is no wonder that local governments demonstrate less and less faith in their state governments.

Cost-Cutting in Rochester

Cutting costs in large old cities with long political histories requires an important mix — namely, a political environment conducive to change and a staff capable of planning and executing cost cuts without destroying the city in the process. A constitutional taxing limit is also a necessary ingredient.

The types of changes made in Rochester during the past four and a half years probably appear trivial to those associated with more technically and professionally advanced cities, but one city's old technology is always another's new one.

When I came to Rochester, three to four sanitation trucks might be going down a street — one or two to collect household waste, one to collect bulk, and one to collect brush and weeds. In addition, two trucks followed each street sweeper. They reported to different organizational chiefs. Some worked on hourly rates, some on daily rates. Some were reflected in the annual budget; others appeared in a separate calendar-year budget prefinanced by borrowing and paid off a year and a half later by special assessment charges based on front footage.

The two budgets were consolidated and put on the same fiscal year. The number of trucks was reduced from 96 to 64, the number of positions from 697 to 360. The annual personnel savings alone, without counting equipment, borrowing, and operation and maintenance charges, amounts to $4.9 million. Citizen complaints, by the way, dropped from 36,700 in 1973 to 19,900 in 1977 despite the cutbacks in staff and equipment.

Other cost reductions and productivity improvements have not been as spectacular. More prudent debt management policies have reduced expensive borrowing for routine equipment replacement, annual road maintenance, and tax and revenue anticipation notes. Annual budget deficits were also ended, eliminating unnecessary borrowing costs.

All city parking garages, previously operated by municipal personnel exclusively, are now on contract, at an estimated net savings of $267,000 per year. A contract to operate the municipal arena and exhibition hall was just executed, producing immediate savings and guaranteeing elimination of a $400,000 annual operating deficit in two years when the city will begin sharing in the profits of the contractor. Contracts have also yielded considerable savings in other labor-intensive areas such as curb and walk laying, street resurfacing, and grave digging, but the real payoffs have been in improved services and completion of work on time.

Savings can also be obtained through improved intergovernmental cooperation. Rochester, for instance, obtains its water by gravity flow from an upland system that extends many miles south of the city. It also pumps water uphill from Lake Ontario. The Monroe County Water Authority until 1971 supplied water directly to a portion of the city as well as to the suburbs. In that year, in fulfillment of a political campaign promise to equalize water rates for all city residents, an agreement was signed between the two water agencies. It was unsatisfactory for the city in many ways. For example, the agreement had the city paying $ .36 per thousand gallons of water bought from the authority but receiving only $ .24 per thousand for city water sold to the authority.

Both the city and the authority owned water-treatment plants side by side in the neighboring town of Greece. The city paid over $400,000 per year in property taxes to Greece while the authority, being exempt by state law, paid nothing. Every year, to no avail, the city submitted legislative bills to rectify what it considered a discriminatory practice.

This year the city and authority agreed to a new contract that will save the city $5.3 million over the next ten years, primarily by equalizing the water exchange rates and transferring the city's water plant to the authority. They also agreed to share the costs of capital improvements to the upland system, thereby eliminating future duplication of effort by the two systems, a major long-term accomplishment for the entire metro area.

Because the city ran out of landfill space and other towns in Monroe County refused to accept city garbage in their landfills, the city began several years ago hauling garbage a round-trip distance of 105 miles. Three years ago Monroe County took over responsibility for solid waste disposal. The annual savings to the city amounted to $1.1 million. The important point is that the responsibility was placed at the government level that has the power to condemn space for waste disposal if it has to and the power to eliminate a 105-mile round trip if it wants to.

Effecting cost reductions in public safety services presents great difficulties to local government officials. The practice of using the same number of patrol assignments on three shifts around the clock, regardless of the incidence of crime or calls for assistance, prevailed when I came to Rochester. Cutting the number of two-person patrol cars, reevaluating the need for sworn officers on inside jobs, and reducing cars assigned to less busy hours allowed the number of sworn officers on duty during the peak evening call hours to be expanded two and a half times by the addition of an overlapping fourth platoon.

Space does not permit discussion of other cost reduction efforts or of the difficulties of bringing about change in fire prevention and suppression. The fire cost battle in Rochester goes under the code name Operation Spot, which not only means we're on the spot, but stands for a problem that is 25 percent social, 25 percent political, 25 percent organizational, and 25 percent tradition.

The key element in most of these cost-saving vignettes is that government personnel costs in New York in some instances have risen high enough that private entrepreneurs can take over public operations and still make a profit, particularly in labor-intensive endeavors.

This is evident in both the parking and auditorium cases. Rochester almost contracted for waste collection in one small sector of the city. However, on the eve of the contract signing, the union proposed that it could do the job less expensively if the city reduced the crew size throughout the city from four to three. Since this was an offer we could not refuse, the contract was not awarded.

Contracting may not always be the answer to cost problems. Capital-intensive operations, such as street lighting, may prove less expensive under full or even partial public ownership depending primarily on how heavily utilities are taxed and the differential between public and private borrowing rates. Few municipal personnel have a sophisticated understanding of how private utility street lighting rates are set and therefore miss opportunities to reduce long-term costs.

Municipalities should avoid contracting for services when the private sector has few strong competitors and there is suspicion of price fixing in the industry. The public interest is not served well by either private or public monopolies.

A major factor in Rochester's labor costs has been payments to the state pension plan. Only recently the state law was changed to require new employees to contribute a portion of their pension payments. Previously the pension plans were noncontributory; the city made the whole payment. State officials are likely to say that it was the action of local officials that resulted in a noncontributory public employee pension system. They will point out that a variety of options are available and that it is not the state's fault that the city chose the most expensive. (Pensions and Social Security taxes total 14 percent of the city and school district budget and 45 percent of the total tax levy.)

Moreover the state's policy of dangling an assortment of options before potential municipal buyers is what I refer to as the magnet approach to state mandates. The most lucrative option sets up a magnetic field that municipal officials have to fight to avoid being sucked into it. The problem is that the magnetic field also acts on the employee unions. The idea that local officials should be able to withstand union demands when state officials put them in the middle is pure bunk. State legislatures and now Congress must give up the direct mandate and magnet mandate approaches unless they are willing to take the responsibility for raising the funds to finance them.

Political style plays a significant part in these cost-cutting stories. As municipal employees move out of the city, they lose their political clout with local elected officials. But the 2 percent constitutional tax margin undoubtedly helped strengthen the Rochester council's resistance to union pressure, permitting layoffs and outside contracting of services which had been rare in the past.

The unfortunate contract that was negotiated between the city and the water authority in 1971 occurred because of a political campaign promise made before analyzing what the contract would cost. Local governments attempting to operate under tight expenditure and tax restrictions cannot afford many decisions like that. Proposition 13 will affect political rhetoric and will force candidates for office, as well as bureaucrats, to do their homework.

The massive savings in waste collection could not have been achieved without the city's ability to regain control of the field force from union domination. I want to focus on the inclusion of supervisors in the union, in particular. Before we could make any dent in the waste-collection cost problem, we needed records on production and time. When the supervisors were asked to supply that information, we had a minor job action and a grievance that went to arbitration. "Not in the job specs," they said.

In a Proposition 13 era state governments must not force their local jurisdictions to fight costs with one arm tied behind their backs. If governments are to be businesslike, then supervisory personnel must be eliminated from union coverage, as in industry. This is another example of how state mandates, even if they do not force direct expenditures on locals, can indirectly contribute to a collusive system, capable of adding immeasurably to the cost of running local government.

These cases reveal that a major problem in cost cutting is the giveaway of such managerial rights as the ability to determine how work should be performed and the resources to be allocated. Fortunately Rochester has not given away too many of these rights, but many places have agreed to union demands for fixed manning schedules, prohibition against use of contracts, and similar rigidities that severely restrict management's ability to manage. Many of these giveaways occurred in the early days of collective bargaining before local officials knew what a labor contract was or who or what management is.

In a Proposition 13 era state municipal collective bargaining laws must be amended to restore the management rights given away by incompetent or collusive officials in the early years of collective bargaining and to remove other impediments to local cost control. State-administered civil service systems need to be reevaluated and changed when they are hampering the timely hiring of qualified personnel and restricting the removal of incompetents. I say this (by the way, I started out as a government labor organizer) not to antagonize or disparage governmental workers but to focus on the fact that a Proposition 13-type lid on taxation leaves little margin for error. Everybody will have to pull his or her own weight.

Meeting the cost problem in local government is not just an issue of personnel management, nor is city hall necessarily the locus for decision making to accomplish appropriate fiscal and management solutions. For communities such as Rochester that have made concerted efforts to reduce costs, it does not take new wisdom to realize that there are limits to what technology can accomplish in the way of cost reductions; that there comes a point when the county and neighboring jurisdictions cannot get the votes to take over any more city services and thus relieve city costs; and that the public does not want to pay any more new service charges and assessments or indirectly to pick up the tab for new charges against the traditionally tax-exempt institutions. Further, at some point cutting services becomes counterproductive to the city's efforts to retain and attract taxpaying residents and employers.

So what do we do about it? One might easily slip into the comfortable position of asking what the federal government is going to do about it. The federal government can and should play a role in the ultimate solutions that this new tax and spending reform spirit will generate directly and indirectly, but the real answers have to come from the grass roots, from the private sector, from the involvement of local government statesmen and professionals, and from academia.

How these voices are organized and deployed and how expeditiously they pursue their missions on a state-by-state basis will determine whether the outcome of the new reform spirit leans toward the baby-out-with-the-bathwater end of the spectrum or closer to the middle ground. I do not believe that the Proposition 13 movement can be stopped through appeals to the heart and good will as those at the other end of the spectrum believe; it is not a feasible alternative in this volatile atmosphere.

Guidelines for Restricting Local Fiscal Powers

For those who are already charging to the barricades to take up battle stations and are now a little confused as to who the enemy

is and what the cause is, let me review, clarify and formulate a set
of principles regarding a middle-ground position.

1. Restrictions on local taxation and spending should be viewed
    primarily as incentives to contain costs and to consider
    alternative approaches to the traditional methods of de-
    livering services; the view that they should be rigid to punish
    naughty bureaucrats distorts the issue and could result in
    a boomerang effect on the taxpayers themselves.

2. Restrictions on local government taxing and expenditures
    should be uniform across all units of government within a
    state consistent with the principle of fair and equal treat-
    ment for all. When this does not occur, as in New York
    State, there is little incentive for the people living in places
    without limits to work legislatively for municipal fiscal
    reforms. Furthermore the areas without tax limits become
    havens for central city escapees desiring better services.
    The Jarvis-Gann approach, from a Rochester perspective,
    at least treats all governmental units the same way.

3. Restrictions should never be imposed without safety valves
    or circuit breakers which allow some kind of cavalry to
    come to the rescue in time. Statewide referenda, long con-
    stitutional amendment processes, and supermajority votes
    are too cumbersome and time-consuming to allow a small
    city to provide improvements that will allow a chocolate
    factory to move into town and thereby increase its tax
    base. If the state government votes rigid limits not related to
    inflation, it should at the same time vote remedies and pro-
    cedures that would be activated when the limit is reached —
    for example, the shifting to alternative revenue sources, the
    transfer of services to the state or other jurisdictions, or the
    consolidation of one unit of government with another.

4. Before placing fiscal restrictions on local governments,
    states should require *state mandate impact statements*
    (SMIS). These statements should inventory both the direct
    mandates and the magnet mandates that a community has
    absorbed and what the costs are to the community. To be
    fair to the state, the SMIS should list new revenues provided

to the locality by the state since each mandate was voted. However, changes in local revenues and the growth of inflation must also be factored in. On the basis of the SMISs, states should be adopting measures to eliminate future mandates that do not carry state appropriations and finding remedies for past decisions that have contributed to local fiscal woes.

Given these principles, it would seem appropriate for states embarking on systematic control over local fiscal matters to set up an organization that would study and evaluate the intergovernmental system on a continual basis. The purpose of such an organization would be to assure the most appropriate assignment of functions among units, the distribution of revenues according to equitable formulas, the identification of opportunities for cost savings through intergovernmental cooperation, and the investigation of ways to better dovetail program and fiscal efforts with the federal government. To a certain extent, such an organization would be a state version of the Advisory Commission on Intergovernmental Relations, established on a bipartisan basis to report to the governor, legislature, local governments, and the public at the same time.

No such mechanism exists in the state of New York. There are always ad hoc commissions assigned to various problems, but these represent fragmented, temporary efforts at best. The mode is generally to respond to problems, whereas what is needed is full-time, continuing research that anticipates problems and attempts to avoid or mitigate them.

Whether a state restricts local fiscal powers or not, a research mechanism of this type, particularly in large, complex states such as New York, is important. When a state imposes fiscal straitjackets on local governments, it must assume greater responsibility for making local government work. This responsibility cannot be exercised competently without ongoing research and related educational efforts. The erratic and pathetic behavior of the New York state legislature in responding to the tax-limit problems of Rochester and other jurisdictions is strong testimony for the need for such a research mechanism. No one can guarantee that the research will be used, but no major corporation today can stay in business very long without a permanent research and development program.

If New York State created such a body, it would have no short-age of work, because no organization is looking at the following current pending issues as a whole.

A recent state lower court decision declaring the local proper-ty tax inappropriate for supporting public education.

Alternative revenues or solutions for Rochester when the service charges and assessments recently authorized by the state legislature expire in two years.

Plans to assist localities to comply with a recent state law requiring all property to be revaluated at 100 percent of market value by 1981.

The city of Rochester's current challenge of the New York state constitution's tax-limit provisions in the U.S. Supreme Court and its relevance to future tax-limit efforts. This court case acknowledges that while California's situation applies equally to all locales across the state, New York's restrictions discriminate against particular jurisdictions.

Rochester's legal action against a proposed mammoth sub-urban shopping center and its significance to taxing and econo-mic development policies. This litigation responds to the lack of a mechanism for distributing property tax revenues on a metro-politan basis and the need for applying regional criteria when considering the relative merits of economic development pro-posals.

Recommendations by a local state senator that the state assume support of public education while full social service funding is picked up by the federal government, thereby freeing the property tax for property-related services only.

I have discussed one viewpoint about state restrictions on local fiscal powers and municipal cost cutting in general. I have not specified a role for the federal government other than to caution against imposing mandates that restrict local government fiscal resources and management flexibility.

The federal government itself is not escaping attack in this spreading tax revolt. Some might say that Washington will have its hands full just coping with its own tax and economy issues and that because presumably there will be fewer increases and possibly some real dollar decreases.

I think there are some major accomplishments of the Wisconsin Civil Service Reform law.

The first major accomplishment — and this caused the biggest fight in the legislature — was to roll back the civil service merit coverage for division administrators. In other words, these administrators were declassified and taken out of the civil service. A division administrator is the person reporting directly to the secretary of a cabinet department. Obviously, a secretary of a cabinet department is a gubernatorial appointee confirmed by the senate. Below the secretary were the line division administrators, and they were civil service appointees.

Wisconsin had a major fight about declassifying them. There were the usual charges that the bureaucracy was being politicized and that the job satisfactions of serving in a merit system were being reduced, and so on and so forth.

Eventually all division administrators will be declassified, beginning next year when the new governor is sworn in.

From the perspective of Proposition 13, the real advantage of declassifying division administrators, who on the federal level would be bureau chiefs, is that they are being made directly responsible to the governor and the gubernatorial appointees. Thus if any future governor is elected on a Proposition 13-type campaign platform requiring serious budget cuts, Wisconsin citizens will know that the bureaucrats have to be responsive to the governor, who has a public mandate. There will be no civil service protection enabling the bureau chiefs to block the governor.

Clearly, having division administrators who are responsive to the governor does not mean the whole bureaucracy will jump. But the question of responsiveness to an elected governor with a public mandate is an important segment of improving personnel management in a post-Proposition 13 world.

The second major accomplishment of civil service reform concerns position requirements. Wisconsin tried to revolutionize the approach to the requirements for filling positions so that in a sense position requirements can be downgraded if necessary and filled with people who need to be paid less to do the same job.

First, the civil service reform bill prohibited across-the-board requirements for general classifications. Instead, the bill said, every job requirement cannot be a general classification requirement but has to be job related. In other words, the person writing the specs and the job description has to justify every requirement as being more than helpful. They have to justify the specs based on job-related needs for that specific job. I think that this requirement is going to be a major accomplishment in reversing a real trend toward credentialism, creeping requirements, and creeping upgrading of jobs.

In addition, the legislation specifies that a college degree can be required only if that degree is required for practicing that profession and for obtaining a license for practicing that profession in the state of Wisconsin.

In other words, to be an M.D., a doctor, and to get a medical license, one must have a college education and medical degree. Thus a state job that requires medical activity can require an M.D. By way of contrast, Wisconsin does not license social workers. Therefore a B.S.W. or an M.S.W. can no longer be required for a social worker position. I think that the removal of credentials is going to have a major effect in cheapening the cost of certain jobs.

Finally, one provision — and I am glad the legislature included it, because of the movement toward recognizing women's contributions to society as volunteers — is that volunteer and unpaid work experience is to be qualified as work experience when an applicant submits a resume based on a job spec. I think that was a good step forward.

The bill contains two provisions regarding supervisors. First, it expanded the mandatory probationary period for supervisors from six months to one year, so that there is a better chance to see whether a supervisor is working out. If not, the supervisor can be bumped and won't have any tenure in the supervisory position. Second, a mandatory training program was added for all new supervisors. This marks a good step forward.

The bill emphasizes filling positions through in-house recruiting. Wisconsin has a job freeze right now imposed by the incumbent acting governor. It will be easier to meet the needs of state government without having to recruit from the outside. And if Wisconsin it will have little time to deal with Proposition 13 and its effects as part of a federal urban policy.

I hope that does not occur, because the caps being placed on local taxing and expenditures will probably have only a minimal effect on the demand for services. Demands that can no longer be met by local governments will filter upward to the state level and to the federal government. The federal government should anticipate these demands and improve its capability to sort them out. Measures of local tax effort and local need should be refined and developed to help formulate federal aid policies that will equalize the effect of varying state restrictions on local taxing and spending and to encourage states to take greater initiative and responsibility in solving local government problems.

Anticipating demands and being prepared for them are not the same as jumping into the act. The federal government can be more effective as a responder than as an initiator. If the demand for federal intervention becomes loud and clear, it will be from a broad segment of the country, not just cities. And with the bottom line being relief of the property tax, the opportunity for tying in federal support with significant reform of the intergovernmental system would be at hand. The national economy benefits little from a fragmented governmental sector, as we attempt to stay competitive in the world marketplace.

Personnel Management in Wisconsin

Mordecai Lee

Wisconsin's biennial budget is $10 billion, and the surplus at the end of the biennium is expected to be a little under half a billion. So the overage is about 5 percent. That overage became a big political issue. The legislature decided to use the surplus to finance a one-shot property tax cut, some cash-on-the-barrelhead capital expenditures, some reduction in state debt, a clean water program, some increases in state aids for school systems. The state set aside about $80 million to finance tax reform next year.

There have been some interesting debates about surpluses. There is now a movement for an initiative-referendum, a constitutional amendment to permit initiative referenda. There has been a movement for a constitutional amendment for a link between the state spending levels and personal income. In other words, the state spending would be a percentage of aggregate personal income. And there have been other effects as well.

One effect concerns the Wisconsin Civil Service Reform Act. This bill came actually before Proposition 13. It was passed by the legislature last November, signed by the governor early this year, and has been going into effect through the year in various stages. By September 1978 the bill was about three-quarters into implementation.

The need for civil service reform in Wisconsin was obvious. The last major reform of Wisconsin civil service took place about 1913. The push for civil service reform was not financial. Only about 18 cents of every dollar spent by the state of Wisconsin is for personnel costs, whether for salaries or for fringe benefits. So personnel costs are well under a quarter of every dollar. Instead of being financially motivated, the reform was management motivated. There was a clear recognition that improving the management of government could indirectly reduce the cost of government. And better management could enhance the efficiency of government and the use of resources. On an economy-efficiency scale, one should think of civil service reform as reform that works at efficiency rather than economy. But one can certainly make a valid and not sophist argument that in the long run civil service reform will lead to economies, has a permanent job freeze, the state will be able through attrition and in-house recruiting, to sustain its current service level without maintaining its current size of state employment.

The bill streamlined grievance procedures to reduce the time involved. The employee has thirty days to file, and the Personnel Commission has ninety days after the case is heard to return a decision. The procedure was streamlined and formalized, and a full-time commission to hear the grievances was created, so there will be no conflict of interest. This change is similar to federal legislation. The civil service commission will no longer be both regulatory and adjudicatory. The new procedures are also intended to minimize the amount of time that supervisors spend on grievances. There are many horror stories about supervisors who spend half their time coping with grievances.

The reform bill tried to increase the flexibility of personnel management. First it expanded the categories of nonpermanent employment and non-full-time employment, so that it will be easier to cope with fluctuations, both increases and decreases. All departments now have to submit programs for flex time, for job sharing, for part-time work, and so on.

Finally, it expanded the opportunities for contracting out, for both personnel and general services. This provision should help permit fluctuations and changes in state spending without necessarily affecting service levels.

The bill increased the role of the legislature in the approval of union contracts. Two years ago, after contracts had been signed by the governor, by the governor's team, and by the American Federation of State, County, and Municipal Employees (AFSCME) and they had gone to the legislature for routine approval, the unthinkable happened: the legislature turned down the contracts. The legislature simply felt that they were inadequate.

The civil service reform bill included a section that increases the role of the legislature in determining the state's bargaining position. Now when the contract comes to the legislature, it will be more a legislative product and will better reflect the mood of the legislature.

The bill created a cabinet department for personnel management, so that this function will not be buried far away from the governor, deep inside a department of administration. Instead, there is now a cabinet secretary for employment relations. I think that having this position will help increase and improve personnel management.

All these provisions that I have mentioned are for the state civil service system. But some of the provisions were also mandated for local civil service systems, for county civil service systems, and for some of the larger cities that have civil service systems. The intent was to bring the lower-level governments along with the state in trying to achieve a consistent personnel position.

Finally, the legislature did some relatively miscellaneous things that I am very proud of. Some appear not to have been accomplished on the federal level. First, the legislature eliminated veterans preference points for promotions, so that veterans preference points apply only for an entry-level job. That, surprisingly, did not spark a big fight. For some reason, the veterans' lobby in Madison was not as well organized as the one in Washington.

Next, the legislature expanded the rule of three for certification of eligibles. Usually the highest-ranking three candidates are submitted to a supervisor for interviewing, and one gets appointed. Five constructed rule of five; it can be expanded up to a rule of ten (up to 10 percent of the actual eligibles). If there is a list of 70 who are certified as eligible, then the highest-ranking seven, or the based on 10 percent of the actual eligibles list. If there is a list of 70 who are certified as eligible, then the highest ranking seven, or the top 10 percent, are going to be certified. In that case the rule becomes a rule of seven.

Thus it might be called a rule of five up to a rule of ten, a maximum of ten.

Finally, a veteran who qualifies to be certified because of preference points is added on to the list of eligibles instead of bumping a woman or a minority member, or even a white male. Thus the manager interviews the five to ten usual candidates plus the veterans who deserve to be qualified.

What does this civil service reform have to do with Proposition 13? Civil service reform is one of those issues that does not have much of a constituency. Everybody is for it, but nobody is really fighting for it. The biggest lesson I have learned as an elected official is that a real imbalance, a kind of fatal flaw exists in our current political system. There are too many issues, and there are indeed two sides of an issue, but the two sides of that issue are not adequately represented before the legislators.

Too often I find myself voting on issues with a highly motivated special interest group on one side and the public at large on the other side. The special interest group is directly and personally affected by the proposed legislation, and because of that, they have the motivation to raise money, to hire a good lobbyist, to develop smooth and slick arguments, to be intensely affected, so intensely affected, by the law that it will affect how they vote, how they contribute money, and so on. The public might be adversely affected by the legislation that the special interest group is pushing. They may even know that they would be adversely affected. But the effect is so marginal for many that the public does not mobilize to counterbalance the pressures that elected officials get from a special interest group.

This is a problem that issues such as civil service reform face. On one side in Washington are veterans, who feel very strongly about it; some labor unions, who feel very strongly about some aspects of the bill; other groups — women and minorities, for example — who feel very strongly about some aspects of the bill. On the other side is the public at large. They support civil service reform; it's an attractive idea, and it might reduce their tax burden in the long run, and they are for efficiency. But are they really going to spend the time and effort that the veterans, for example, are going to spend lobbying on the bill?

This imbalance is a major problem for the political system. We do not have a balanced representation, an equal representation, of all the voices that are affected. The special interest groups are represented in almost inverse proportion to their size.

I think Proposition 13 is a terrific event. In the fifties, whenever some do-gooders wanted to do something, they always said it was for national defense. If you wanted a good highway system in the United States, you called it the National Defense Interstate Highway System, and you got it passed. If you wanted aid to higher education, you called it the National Defense Higher Education Act, and so on.

Well now, thanks to Proposition 13, civil service reform can be packaged as Proposition 13 personnel management reform. And with that kind of flag on it, I can't imagine anybody opposing it.

I am suggesting that it is not a fraud to relate civil service reform to improved government. Civil service reform does relate to improved government, although more to the efficiency of government than to the economy of government. And it is important not to promise that civil service reform can do more than it can. But the public mood is obvious.

At a town hall meeting in my district, someone asked me about a sunset bill that was in the legislature. This was just before Proposition 13 passed. I said, Well, I'm for sunset in principle, but the bill that is now being debated by the legislature is a poor bill. And they asked why. I said, It is so poorly drafted that within the first three-year period of the bill, the entire state government would come up for review. If we get clogged up in three years because we didn't have time to act or to review those issues, we might inadvertently abolish the entire state government. And I paused. I thought everybody would say, You're right; we want sunset, but we don't want to over-do it. Instead there was silence, a pause, and then they all applauded. They thought it was terrific that the state government would disappear within three years.

The public mood is negative about government. And I think that legislators should push for civil service reform. I think that management needs more flexibility, that civil service reform can improve the management of government, and that this reform should be packaged as a Proposition 13 response. But we shouldn't over-promise what it can accomplish in the immediate future.

Political Implications of the Taxing and Expenditure Limitation Movement

Philip Burgess

Public initiatives to limit taxes and spending at both the state and local levels have had a range of impacts, including a scramble for funds to rescue threatened services. More important, however, the taxing and expenditure limitation (TEL) movement has raised some fundamental political issues, issues related to the direction of American society and the intrusiveness of government in the lives of people and institutions. The TEL movement raises issues about the relative responsibilities of the public and private (nongovernmental) sectors and the balance of power between the public order and the civic order in a democratic society. The TEL movement raises questions about what services should be provided by what levels of government, a classic and enduring issue in a federal system of government. And the TEL movement raises fundamental questions about the "leaky bucket approach" to financing public services. Arthur Okun describes the leaky bucket as what happens when the federal government takes $4,000 from each of ten affluent families to support forty poor families. In theory, this should provide a $1,000 grant to each low-income family. In fact, as Okun observes, "the program has an unresolved technological problem: the money must be carried from the rich to the poor in a leaky bucket." The poor get significantly less than the $1,000 collected, and the rest waters federal, state, and local bureaucracies, universities, think tanks, and other supporting institutions located beneath the leaking bucket.

Viewed this way, those scrambling for funds to rescue threatened services are probably misreading what the public is saying. The much heralded tax revolt may be related more to issues of governance than to issues of taxation. Indeed, the evidence from opinion surveys, electoral outcomes, and other sources seems to support the proposition that the TEL movement has more to do with reclaiming power (an accountability issue) than with reclaiming money (a taxation issue).

Let's briefly consider the factors that have shaped the current state of affairs. First, government has become a major growth industry, with explosive growth in public sector employment (one of

107

five workers is on a public sector payroll, and public sector workers draw $244 billion in pay and fringes) and in the public sector's share of national income (now nearly 40 percent). Second, the growth in employment and spending has been accompanied by government's increasing assertiveness, intrusiveness, and pervasiveness as both the scope and magnitude of governmental power have increased. Third, the power of government has been increasingly wielded by the "iron triangle" of legislative staffs, agency civil servants, and national, state, and local single-issue lobbying associations — what James Madison called factions. Moreover, the iron triangle is self-serving (review public sector retirement plans), self-perpetuating (review the tenure of legislative and administrative leadership), and vindictive (as nearly every community that has rejected a school bond referendum knows).

Fourth, the factions have largely displaced political parties in the aggregation and articulation of political demands. As a result, political parties are relegated largely to the nominating function in elections and the caucus function in legislatures. Political demands are no longer prenegotiated and integrated through party structures. Instead, single-issue demands are presented directly to the Congress and the administration. As Morris Fiorina, a keen political analyst, has observed, congressmen win coming and going. The congressman initiates new legislation in response to demands and gets credit from the faction for establishing a new program. Agencies then promulgate rules and regulations to give flesh to broadly written legislative mandates. The regulations, however, inevitably trample on people's toes. The trampled constituent then petitions his congressman for help. The congressman, transforming himself from lawmaker to ombudsman, gets more staff to do his case work, thus driving up his visibility and electability back home — and the cost of government. He wins both ways, and the taxpayer loses, a fact that taxpayers are beginning to realize.

Fifth, we have the impact of the federal government's mismanagement of the national economy, and particularly the problems of monetary instability which takes the form of inflation driven by large and recurring federal deficits, excessive regulation (driving up the costs of goods and services and reducing investments in research and development), and the multiple taxation of investment capital

(further straining an already tight capital market). Excessive inflation coupled with progressive tax rates and efficient assessment
systems gave windfall revenues to all levels of government, permitting
legislators to "cut" taxes yet increase their "take" of the public's
wealth. The public has caught on. Not only do individuals take
home smaller paychecks; government has more to hire people at
equivalent pay scales, initiate new programs, and find new areas to
regulate. People are beginning to say no, to reassert the revolutionary
principle that democratic government operates by the consent of
the governed. As a result, the forty-year bull market in government
spending – a period during which both the costs and power of
government ballooned out of control – is coming to an end. Accordingly, the challenge is not a return to normalcy by rescuing
threatened services and restoring traditional privileges but a reassessment of who needs what services at what level and who can
best provide them. An across-the-board policy to respond to TEL
impacts may be inappropriate, since the differences from area to
area may be more important than their similarities. Indeed, the
ultimate impact must come at the federal level where more than
three-fourths of our money is collected and spent.

The problems we face today serve to underscore the wisdom we
might have had in the past by taking more seriously the results of
the continuing appraisals by the Advisory Commission on Intergovernmental Relations (ACIR), by the General Accounting Office
(GAO), and by others. Recommendations resulting from this process
of continuing policy analysis and systematic evaluation have been
largely ignored – recommendations calling for more tax indexation, better methods of assessing property taxes, stronger requirements for local government to give full disclosure for property
taxes, recommendations against the mandating habits of higher units
of government, particularly the federal government. The problems
we face today exist primarily because we have ignored those pleas
from the past, pleas accompanied by carefully laid recommendations.

As a result, there are two major political implications of the
TEL movement. One is the likely reprivatization of many public
services in many state and local communities. Many think this
process will increase the capacity of the public sector to serve the

public interest on the grounds that the public sector cannot serve the public interest if it is a principal provider — because a provider cannot also be a referee. Still others believe that reprivatization is not likely to be sensitive to the needs of the less privileged underclasses.

The second major political implication is the move toward institutional rearrangements, especially in the intergovernmental arena, and the reassignment of functions and responsibilities. The role of different stakeholders in our society, and particularly different levels of government, is being reexamined. Here we face the real danger of further centralizing power at higher levels of government: more centralization at the state level vis-a-vis local units of government (generally an undesirable development) and more centralization within the federal government (equally undesirable).

There are nine principal responses to be considered by our national leadership in the Congress, the administration, and in state houses and courthouses for, indeed, state and local elected leadership are also part of our national leadership cadre.

First, an intergovernmental partnership requires strong and robust entities at each level. We cannot let efforts to limit taxes and spending lead to greater centralization of power, either within states or within the federal system at the federal level.

Second, more serious consideration should be given to the indexation of income and other taxes, so that the proportion of taxes paid cannot be artificially increased by inflation or other forms of monetary instability.

Third, I believe we should take seriously recommendations by the ACIR regarding the spotlighting of revenue increases; that is, establishing procedures at all three levels of government requiring clear and explicit signals that a legislative body — the Congress, the state legislature, or the city council — is going to increase revenues. The Florida example is often cited.

Fourth, national leadership should affirm the proposition that higher levels of government have an obligation to reimburse lower levels of government for the full cost of implementing policies, programs, and directives originating with higher levels. Indeed, the history of this country, particularly over the last fifteen years, provides example after example of the federal government's imposition on state and local governments (and state government's imposition on local government) of policies, programs, and administrative requirements whose costs the higher levels are not paying and are not willing to pay. Consider, for example, the $2.5 billion arbitrary funding ceiling established in 1972 on the Federal Public Assistance Program (Title XX), costing state and local governments more than $4 billion. We have a similar situation in the Indochina refugees area. The federal government has mandated a humanitarian program, which most Americans would support, for Vietnamese and Cambodian refugees; yet the federal government is pulling out of the program, leaving a few state and local governments substantial responsibility for supporting that federal policy.

At the state and local level, we find case after case of severe, state-imposed restrictions on revenue-generating and administrative procedures in the cities, yet the states are not willing to pay the costs of those restrictions. So we must stop higher levels of government from initiating new programs, mandating their continuation, and pulling out, leaving lower levels of government (with greatly restricted revenue sources) holding the bag and failing to live up to the old obligations. In short, some form of fiscal impact analysis, not too complicated, is needed to accompany major legislation and major regulations.

Fifth, we should reconsider federal formulas that reward state and local governments with high taxes. We should encourage, not penalize, state and local governments that reduce or rationalize the tax burdens of their citizens.

Sixth, state executives who oppose increasing the role of state legislatures in the appropriation of federal funds may want to re-examine their opposition. Indeed, greater involvement of legislators at the state level in examining the income and the programs (and the future commitments) spawned by federal dollars may lead to more accountability. The bureaucratic guild system linking technocrats at all three levels bypasses the elected leadership in both the legislative and executive branches.

Seventh, national leadership ought to do everything possible to revive interest in and foster a national debate over a constitutional amendment to peg revenue sharing at a fixed percentage (say, 20 percent) of federal revenues. That issue has been discussed, sometimes seriously, sometimes not so seriously; but it is an issue that deserves serious consideration if we are to rationalize our systems for collecting and spending revenues. While the federal income tax system is efficient, most problems requiring resources are found at the state and local levels.

Eighth, since major public management problems at the state and local levels are caused by the policies and administrative practices of the federal government itself, the national leadership should foster the political and legislative basis for (1) reorienting federal domestic programs to minimize the mandated but unsupported administrative burdens on state and local government and the conflicts with local priorities; (2) expanding and coordinating federal public management assistance aimed specifically at strengthening the overall management capacity of state and local governments desiring such assistance; and (3) improving the federal government's machinery for conducting intergovernmental business in order to bring about more effective state and local participation and liaison.

Finally, we need to revise our textbooks in public administration. Many of these textbooks teach young public administrators that the expansion of the public sector is one of their professional responsibilities. At the least, that view ought to be balanced with a contrary view — that liberty, equity, and solvency require curtailing the growth and intrusiveness of the public sector.

Tax Reform and Proposition 13

James M. Savarese

California's Proposition 13 is easily understood and easily explained. It is a response to a total breakdown of political responsibility in the state of California.

A clear understanding of Proposition 13's origins is essential to an analysis of its significance. Most of the circumstances surrounding passage of the Jarvis-Gann initiative were unique to California. Home owners in California were caught in an inflationary squeeze. As property values skyrocketed, so did property tax bills. In many cases the inflated value of a family's property was totally out of line with its current income. Many could no longer afford the taxes on their property. Some were forced to sell. At the same time that the results of an inequitable tax were being so painfully felt, Californians witnessed the accumulation of an unprecedented surplus in the state coffers, over $5 billion. This combination of factors created intense pressure for relief at almost any price.

The danger inherent in the initiative-referendum method of implementing legislative change was forcefully demonstrated in California. California's real need was for tax reform. Because well-financed private interests were able to manipulate the initiative process, the result was an unnecessarily broad and drastic tax and spending cut. In addition to a one-time cut in property tax revenues, the amendment limits future property tax increases to 2 percent per year. With inflation exceeding 8 percent per year and the cost of providing public services increasing, Proposition 13 is aptly termed a meat-axe approach.

As property taxes were rolled back to 1 percent of market value, local governments in California, including school districts, lost $7 billion in revenues. The irony is that only one-third of this total tax relief went to home owners, nothing went to renters, and nearly $5 billion was handed out to commercial and business interests.

The bad features of Proposition 13 would never have passed the state legislature. The initiative process, appealing to many as directly expressing the wishes of the people, is even more amenable to manipulation by special interests than the legislative process.

The results of Proposition 13 are now beginning to be realized. As expected, most jurisdictions have had to implement cutbacks. The short-run picture, however, is not nearly so bleak as the longer-run. The legislature enacted a bail-out program to redistribute $5 billion of the state surplus to localities to replace lost property tax revenues. This action mitigates the threat of drastic service cutbacks, although most jurisdictions must still cut their budgets by about 10 percent. The exceptional state surplus took several years to accumulate; it is now being depleted rapidly, and it is unlikely that California will be able to build it up again to the level required to replace lost local revenue.

Proposition 13 does not mean that the people of California were trying to limit government spending in California. In fact, the people of California, against a background of political irresponsibility, did not believe that services would be cut. There are no data to show that Californians, when they voted for Proposition 13, thought that they were voting to cut services. They did not believe that they were in effect cutting services, because there was a $5 billion surplus. And they knew that if taxes are cut $6 billion and $5 billion is in the state treasury and a couple of hundred million is in county governments, then there is no reason to have a cutback in services.

The political irresponsibility about Proposition 13 included forecasts of gloom and doom about a quarter of a million public employees being laid off. Public employees never believed that, and they were the people whose life was on the line. Between the passage of Proposition 13 and the first week in September (1978), there were twenty-four thousand layoffs in California. Almost all the cutbacks were in the schools, but this happens every year because the schools shut down in the summer, and many people are temporarily laid off. That is what happened in California.

There were some real cutbacks. There were some cutbacks in services. Some library hours were shortened. Schools were shut down. Summer schools were cut back in several cities. Clearly something happened as a result of Proposition 13. But what happened must be put in perspective.

What is the implication of California's experience for other places? A major political challenge is containing the cost of government. One of the most important political challenges that confront politicians is dealing with the tax structure of state and local governments in a responsible fashion.

The problem of tax reform has still not been adequately addressed in California; in fact, the state is now stuck with an even more unworkable tax system. The role of the property tax has been greatly diminished as an important element of the state's tax system, and valuable flexibility has been lost. There are many methods for making different elements in the state tax structure more progressive. It is not necessary, and indeed may be undesirable, to scrap major portions of the system.

There is a lesson in the California experience for other states who are preparing to jump on the Proposition 13 bandwagon. Only the state surplus is preventing disastrous cutbacks in services in California, and other states do not have this short-term cushion. Moreover, Proposition 13 does not address the fundamental problem of necessary tax reform. Those who voted for Proposition 13 were calling for property tax relief in an unworkable tax system. What they got was a potentially huge reduction in public services accompanied by massive windfall gains to big businesses.

Wisconsin, Minnesota, and Hawaii have done excellent jobs with their tax structures. But they do not have Proposition 13-type movements. Why? The reason is simple. The people in those states generally desire a high level of public services. But they think that, on balance, everybody is paying their fair share for them.

States where Proposition 13 fever is spreading — Michigan, Massachusetts, and Illinois, for example — have a flat-rate income tax. These are the places that have the most action on a Proposition 13.

What is a fair share? Reasonable people can disagree about what a fair and equitable tax structure is. But I think there are three principles of tax equity that most people would agree on.

First, states have to have graduated income taxes. If a state does not have a graduated income tax as the basic way of financing government, the state is in trouble. If it is not in trouble now, it will be in a few years, because a graduated income tax is the mechanism for ensuring a sophisticated, well-funded state revenue-sharing program, in which states pay for services that local governments should not be funding.

Take welfare, for example. In New York State local governments pick up 25 percent of the aid for dependent children program and 25 percent of Medicaid costs. Scandalous. Welfare should be a state responsibility. County governments should not be paying for welfare. Why should a big part of property taxes, which should be paying for municipal services, go to welfare payments? It is not a county's responsibility to have a large welfare population. They did not encourage the immigration of people to that county. Welfare is a state function, at least; it is probably a federal function. But it is certainly not a local function.

Welfare financing is a problem in New York City. New York City has financial problems because it has a billion dollars in welfare and Medicaid bills every year. No other big city in the United States has that kind of responsibility. Chicago has no welfare responsibility. Nor does Philadelphia, Boston, or Detroit.

New York City went broke in 1975 — and it was broke. Authorities say New York City did not go bankrupt, but it did. The city was technically in default on its loans. When New York City went bankrupt in 1975, the deficit was $750 million. The city had a billion dollars in welfare payments that year. If New York State were responsible in dealing with its local governments, as other state governments are, New York City would never have been in default. They would have had a surplus, a $200 million surplus in 1975, which was not the best year economically.

Second, when states raise sales taxes they ought to provide sales tax relief. Connecticut's 7 percent sales tax is irresponsible. Many states exempt food from the base of the sales tax. I don't think that is appropriate. I don't think that I ought to be able to escape paying four cents on the dollar when I buy sirloin steaks. Everybody should pay the sales tax. But there should be a rebate through a sales tax credit mechanism of some kind. There should be a way to provide sales tax relief without losing a lot of revenues from people who really should be paying sales tax.

Third, and probably most important now, is the property tax. If Proposition 8 had been put on the ballot last year, or if the legislature had passed it without putting it on the ballot, there would have been no Proposition 13.

Proposition 13 was a $2.5 billion tax cut for residential home owners. Proposition 8 was a $2.5 billion tax cut for residential home owners and renters. Why would Californians choose to give $4.5 billion of relief to the Arco Towers in Los Angeles or to the California Power and Electric Company and the telephone company? If the people of California had believed their political leaders when they said that the biggest beneficiary of Proposition 13 would be California Power and Electric Company, they would not have voted a $128 million savings for the utility. No legislature could have passed something like that. One that tried would have been run out of town on a rail, even out of Sacramento.

The positive side of Proposition 13 is that it is property tax relief funded at the state level by a sophisticated circuit breaker mechanism. That is the only way to get property tax relief. Rolling back the rate to 1 percent or 1.5 percent, as they are trying to do in Idaho and Oregon, is not the way. Why should someone with an income of $400,000 living in a $2 million mansion pay 1 percent of the value of his property in property taxes? That person should pay full freight. But in California a person making $15,000, $20,000 a year who bought a home for $40,000 three years ago now has a home worth $125,000 because of inflated property values. That person has now to pay $3,000 a year in property taxes. It's irresponsible to think that a person making $15,000 or $20,000 can afford to pay that high a tax. So a circuit breaker program, funded at the state level, is put in to take care of that problem. This mechanism is not magic. Many states — Wisconsin, Minnesota, Michigan — have circuit breaker programs.

In summary, the average taxpayer pays nearly one-third of his or her taxes to state and local government. Of these taxes, the property tax is the largest single source of revenue. Income taxes rank fourth in importance, behind federal aid and sales taxes.

Equity is the essential consideration in devising a workable tax system. With few exceptions, tax levies should be based on ability to pay. It is the absence of equity in taxation that leads to Proposition 13-type actions.

State and local taxes are in general regressive, relying heavily on property and sales taxes. The property tax as currently administered is one of the most regressive taxes levied by any government. The irony here is that the property tax is potentially one of the most progressive revenue raisers in state and local finance. This is the only major tax in our country that is levied directly on accumulated wealth and unrealized capital gains income. Many wealthy people have little taxable income, as a result of special preferences in the IRS code. Soundly structured and fairly administered, the property tax could be a progressive, loophole-free source of income.

A circuit breaker mechanism, which would grant tax relief based on income and property tax level, is the best option available to state and local governments to ease the property tax burden. It can be well targeted to low- and middle-income taxpayers, thus preserving a primary source of local revenue without sacrificing an equitable tax structure.

A sound state tax system should be a balanced combination including a good progressive income tax, a property tax with well-designed circuit breaker provisions, and tax credits for sales tax relief. The principle of tax equity must be a foremost consideration.

The Taxpayer Revolt: An Opportunity to Make Positive Changes in Local Government

Selma J. Mushkin, Frank H. Sandifer
Charles L. Vehorn, Charlie G. Turner

There has been an almost steady outpouring of analyses and reports in recent months on the immediate effects and consequences of Proposition 13 and other taxpayer rebellions. As is often the case, the published reports on the phenomena have been almost as fascinating as the events they purport to analyze. We have seen, for example, dire predictions of dreaded consequences from Proposition 13, rosy predictions of beneficial consequences, and middling predictions of muddled consequences — some good effects and some bad effects that may offset one another.

This paper is not another analysis of Proposition 13's effects. Nor is it an assessment of whether the tax-cutting movement exemplified by California's Proposition 13 is either good or bad for the country. Rather, it starts from the recognition that Proposition 13 is already law in California and that there are now or will be tax cuts, tax limitations, or spending ceilings in other states as well. Thus this paper begins with the fait accompli of Proposition 13 and addresses the question how local governments will respond to their changed circumstances.

The taxpayers' revolt, as it is frequently called, provides the occasion to take a hard look at some governmental options that may not have been considered seriously enough before. It also provides a strong impetus to make changes in the way local governments operate. For example, it will necessitate even better management of governments, particularly better management of government work forces. Furthermore the tax-reduction movement provides an incentive to revise the financing of government services. General taxes such as the property tax are a valuable means of producing needed government revenues. However, in many cases alternatives such as user fees and charges can be fairer and allow more citizen involvement in determining what services should be produced, in what quantities, with what qualities, and at what cost.

We wish to present some of these alternatives to offset the budgetary game playing that can and frequently does occur in governmental decision making. Any substantial reduction in taxes or budgets is likely to bring much overreaction as well as under-reaction. Some government officials will want to take immediate and drastic steps to cut costs, steps that will have severe negative effects on vital services. Others will want to do nothing in the hope that the cuts will be restored; they may delay action so long that many valuable alternatives become unfeasible.

In the federal government there is a well-known budget process sometimes called the Washington Monument Game. The name is taken from the archetypal ploy, attributed to the National Park Service, of outlining politically undesirable consequences of proposed budget cuts — in this case, suggesting that the first step the Park Service would take to accommodate a lower budget level would be to close the Washington Monument to visitors. The monument is, of course, a prime attraction to visitors, most of whom are the constituents of the congressmen who must vote on the budget. Some local government officials in the debate preceding passage of Proposition 13 in California demonstrated their acumen for this game. There were plenty of hints and outright claims that police, fire, and education services would be drastically curtailed. The whole idea in this game is to suggest to the voters that their actions will result in the curtailment or elimination of the services they are likely to consider most vital.

The following sections of this paper will discuss some of the alternatives available to government managers and elected officials in responding to citizen demands for reduced taxes. The first section is a general discussion of economic considerations at work in the political process when tax cuts are being forged, as well as some of the economic constraints on governments' responses to tax cuts. The second section focuses on the concept of public prices for public goods, based on the premise that many government services, like private services, can be priced and consumers can signal their demands through purchase of the services. The third section deals with improving the management of local governments' largest operating cost item — personnel — particularly ways that personnel costs might be reduced without resorting to drastic measures such as general layoffs and ways that personnel productivity can be enhanced without substantially increasing revenue demands.

General Economic Considerations Regarding Proposition 13

It is useful to think of the taxes cut through passage of Proposition 13 and other measures in terms of three separate but highly related concepts. First, the cuts represent taxes saved to the citizens who would have had to pay them. Second, they represent reduced revenues, which either are lost completely or must be made up from other sources. Third, they mean reduced expenditures unless the revenues are replaced.

If citizens vote to reduce property taxes, they may be voting for one or more different aspects of tax reduction. They may be voting to reduce public expenditures because they believe the levels of some services are too high given the costs of those services. Such a discrepancy could be caused partly by a lag in adapting services to changes in community needs. The school system may now be larger and consist of more highly trained staff than is required for the reduced number of students. Any institution, public or private, has difficulty accepting and adjusting to adverse conditions. Part of the vote may be against certain local programs that are mandated at a higher level, for example, welfare programs. To the extent that the voters prefer a lower level of services, it is necessary to reevaluate existing programs and, if warranted, adjust them to the desired levels if possible.

Another aspect of the vote for Proposition 13 could be a demand for greater efficiency in government. It is widely believed that government workers are overpaid and underworked. Even if this is not true, those who believe it will probably vote for a tax reduction in the hope that expenditures can be reduced without a proportionate reduction in services. Of course, any organization has some inefficiencies in it; both management and workers become accustomed to performing services in a particular fashion. Proposition 13 may provide the jolt that speeds up changes toward more efficient operation. However, there are limits to the increases in efficiency that can occur within the context of a given technology. Increased intensity of work or smoother coordination of efforts can move government toward efficient operation, but these are likely to be one-time changes rather than the annual productivity changes observed in manufacturing. Nevertheless, in addition to the task of determining where reductions in services should be made, public managers should accept this opportunity to improve the efficiency of local government.

Some voters may support a tax reduction in order to shift the incidence of taxation in a way favorable to them. Some of the voters simply would want to avoid property taxes because they pay a relatively larger share of property taxes than of sales or income taxes. However, many citizens probably believe that too much public service is being provided from general tax revenue. They do not believe that the value they receive from such services is worth the tax share that they pay. Howard Jarvis has stated frequently that property taxes should be used only to finance property-related public services, although his definition of property-related may be narrower than others.

Some public services can be provided through user charges. If such charges were levied on all citizens in a fashion similar to property taxes, then the name would have changed, but presumably citizen desires would not be served. However, if user charges are designed to allow citizens to choose varying levels of service and to allow those receiving the service to pay for it, then a shift to user charges should increase community welfare. The readjustments to Proposition 13 present an opportunity to supply more of the public's desired amount of services through user charges.

DYNAMIC ADJUSTMENT TO REDUCED LEVELS OF PUBLIC EXPENDITURE

Adjustments to expenditure reductions will generally be less efficient in the short run than in the long run. Efficiency means providing a given level of service with the least costly combination of inputs (labor and capital) given the prices of those inputs (rents on capital and wages of labor). Part of the short-run inefficiency is due to extended contract provisions, and some of it is due to nonreversible capital expenditures.

There is some evidence that local government services are produced with technology that yields approximately constant returns to scale.[1] Thus half the service can be provided at half the cost, provided that the service level is known far enough in advance to be efficiently planned. If a city is forced to operate with half the budget but must retain all the capital that was previously efficient, then less than half the previous service can be provided. A simple diagram makes the point (see figure 1).

Figure 1. Production under Reduced Budgets

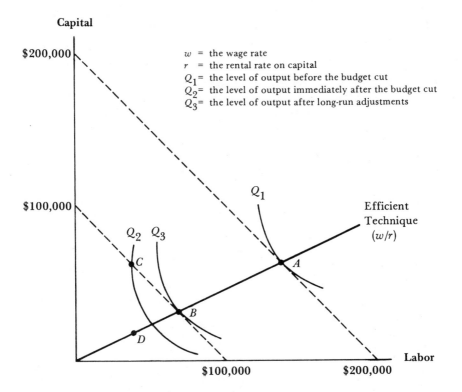

Capital

$200,000

$100,000

$100,000 $200,000   Labor

w = the wage rate
r = the rental rate on capital
Q_1 = the level of output before the budget cut
Q_2 = the level of output immediately after the budget cut
Q_3 = the level of output after long-run adjustments

Q_1

Q_2 Q_3

C

A

B

D

Efficient
Technique
(w/r)

Eventually point B on the figure can be reached (after building and equipment depreciate and are replaced as needed), and service level 3 (Q_3), which is half of service level 1 (Q_1), can be provided at half the cost. However, an initial (unexpected) cut of expenditures from $200,000 to $100,000 would result in point C, which is less efficient and overly capital intensive. If the technology used to produce the service does not allow substitution between capital and labor (the technology has fixed coefficients or fixed proportions of capital and labor), then point D is reached. It uses the initial technique at the level determined by the amount of the most scarce factor, in this case labor. Many economists believe that production technology is largely of the fixed coefficient type once the physical plant and machinery are purchased and set into operation.[2]

Local government produces many different services; some can be produced with differing capital-to-labor ratios, and some are close to the fixed-coefficients model. The first type might be the public library system. Reduced staffing may result in less productive use of the building, equipment, and books, but such nonpersonnel expenses will for the most part still provide benefits to the public. The second type might be the police department. The public receives little benefit from having two hundred cars and only one hundred police officers.

Should the government dispose of the excess equipment and property? Yes, if there is little difference between the disposal price and the price one would have to pay to purchase additional equipment. However, the main adjustment problem is that there is usually a wide gap between purchase price and resale price — for example, between what the city pays for police cars and the price at which it can sell comparable cars. Depending on this price differential, the rate of interest, the maintenance costs, the difference in effectiveness between new and older cars, and the rate of depreciation of police cars, it may be more cost-effective to store unneeded police cars until older ones are retired.

PERSONNEL REDUCTIONS

From a simple efficiency standpoint, government workers (given their pay) who are most efficient to use in the changed circumstances should be retained (or hired) and everyone else let go. However, for contract and other reasons that action is seldom possible; the result is inefficiencies similar to having excess capital. The city may have more senior-level personnel than is efficient. If layoffs are necessary, many of the people who must be retained (because of seniority, for instance) will be paid a higher salary than those who are laid off. These higher-paid personnel may be efficient under normal operations but not necessarily under the new conditions. For example, a fire marshal may be excellent at his usual job of investigating the causes of fires, but he may be less efficient at fire station duty than a lower-paid firefighter.

An additional problem is low morale. When people's livelihood is threatened, they are likely to be depressed and have poorer performance on the job. This reaction may be offset in part by the stimulus to greater effort from the fear of losing one's job, but the net effect is probably negative. In addition, various retaliatory measures (work slowdowns, insolence to the public) may be undertaken by employees as a group or as individuals. This retaliation is most likely if the public employees see the public or public leaders as the enemy.

Such factors are likely to make the effect of a sharp reduction in public expenditures worse than anticipated in the initial stages. A strong argument can be made for a phased reduction in expenditures to the new desired level, even if present levels of spending are too high. In California the state budget surplus has effectively allowed local governments the time to reduce expenditures in a series of steps. If next year's state surplus will be lower but still substantial, the cities and counties have two more years before their budgets must be brought in line with their reduced tax revenues. Of course, this assumes the state will once more distribute its surplus to the local governments. If measures similar to Proposition 13 are adopted in other states or cities, long-term efficiencies will be enhanced if the measures reflect the lack of such large revenue surpluses and make provision for phased reductions in expenditures.

Nevertheless, if immediate reductions are mandated, there are some ways to minimize the adverse effects. All employees should be consulted about available options and asked to express their preferences. Careful analysis of areas of cost reductions to maintain the highest level of service commensurate with the new expenditures level, rather than across-the-board cuts, should help minimize the impact of the reductions.

Action on Revenues: Opportunities for User Charges

There are three major sources of local government revenue: local taxation, intergovernmental grants, and user charges. When the public revolts against property taxes and forces a reduction in that source of revenue, local government officials can reduce their expenditures proportionately, look to higher-level governments for larger grants, establish or raise nonproperty taxes, or place public prices on public products. Not all local government services are amenable to the pricing mechanism. Some public services have a redistributive characteristic; it would be inappropriate to charge the poor for consumption of services designed explicitly for their benefit.[3] Some public services have characteristics that prevent exclusion of nonpayers. Control of communicable diseases and the maintenance of public safety are examples of such services. When beneficiaries can be identified, however, user charges provide a means of rationing government output, while allocating the burden of payment to those desiring the service.[4]

RATIONALE FOR MORE RELIANCE ON USER CHARGES

Most economists have long favored greater emphasis on user fees and charges. Three of the major reasons are the following.[5] (1) They can improve efficiency in choice and public resource allocation. (2) They can improve government structure. (3) They can be more, rather than less, equitable in certain cases.

In each community citizens now express their demands for local public goods through voting. But this mechanism results in a supply of public services that is not sensitive to variations in demand by individual citizens. For example, the interests of the elderly are often different from those of families with young children. Some divergences among individual citizens do not yield efficient outcomes, except in very special circumstances. A price for a public service, in contrast, permits citizens to record their preferences by purchasing the quantity and quality of services desired.

Under present public resource allocation practices, the wrong product is sometimes produced in the wrong quantity and with inappropriate quality differentiation. *Wrong* is used here with the special meaning of different in type, quantity, and quality from that which would be produced if rigorous analysis were made of comparative effectiveness at the given budget level. It is also being used to describe the volume and quality of production that is lower than it would be at market prices under competitive conditions.

Analysis of a public service or activity may give new emphasis to uncertainty about the consumer or voter's response to the public product being produced. If the government sets a price on the product — thereby opening up a market through which consumers can register their vote for or against, by either paying the price or not consuming the product — the price could guide the city in the production of its services.

Local governments are currently structured in ways that centralize authority for spending decisions. But there are many enterprises under the local government umbrella. Conceptually it could be more efficient to decentralize by allowing some enterprises to operate on a fee-for-service basis. This structure would be beneficial to consumers because it would give the government enterprises the opportunity to compete with private enterprises that provide similar services. Such competition should foster greater efficiency.

Decentralization would allow public enterprises to operate as separate entities, generate their own funds through user charges, and place only their profits into the local government general fund. Rates for fire protection, for example, could be based on pricing rules that take into account property value and fire hazards on the property, with lower rates for less hazardous occupancies.[6] Part of the monies paid in as fees could be set aside in a separate account to provide low- or no-interest loans to property owners for improving the fire risk of their structures.

GREATER FAIRNESS

A fee or public price could be a fairer source of revenue than other sources. If prices were used instead of taxes, some poor families might choose not to have the priced services. Analysis of current use of services by income class may disclose a heavy concentration in use by middle-income families. Fairness is a composite effect of payments and services. Many public services such as general aviation airports, museums, libraries, and golf courses are used more by middle-income groups than by the poor. To the extent that zero prices unduly inflate the demand, the tax bill is paid by all taxpayers for services that are used only by some. In this case the low-income families are partially subsidizing the middle-income families under the present financing system. Relative income effects are at issue, as well as the distribution of benefits among age groups.

Prices for services may also become fairer because only those who benefit from the services would pay for them. Prices can be used to discourage some users and to encourage others (for example, by negative prices). If uniform charges are more regressive than an alternative revenue system, it is possible to devise a fair pricing method by use of eligibility tests to determine ability to pay. This method has been used in financing health care service, certain welfare services, such as family counseling, and school meal programs. Such a technique gives the subsidy to those who need it, while making the benefits of the service available to all those who desire to purchase it.

LIMITATIONS TO INCREASING USER CHARGES

One difficulty in extending user charges is that many fiscal officers feel the political constraints are too binding;[7] another is determining the appropriate price to charge. Local policymakers who indicate a political reluctance to extend user charges may be doing so because they are unaware of the potential of public prices. A recent Rand report suggests that policymakers, many of whom have been schooled in the judiciary process, are more familiar with regulation as a tool.[8] However, public pricing can alter people's behavior, perhaps even more efficiently than regulation. For example, charging for a public service can discourage misuse of that service. A good illustration is the fees for emergency ambulance services that some local governments, including the District of Columbia, now impose. The fee discourages requests for ambulances in situations that are not really emergencies.

Once a decision is made to rely more on public pricing, the next complication is establishing the appropriate price for a given service.[9] When a price less than the appropriate price is charged, a subsidy is given to the person purchasing the service. The Advisory Commission on Intergovernmental Relations has suggested that states provide consultants and technical assistance to local governments to determine the appropriate price to charge. However, many states currently do not have the capability to offer sound advice on the pricing of public services.[10] Even with this limitation, it would be possible to set a price, assess demand, and then reset the price if the first price was inappropriate. This incremental procedure could help in overcoming the difficulties in determining price elasticities for public goods.

Although there are obstacles to more reliance on public pricing, municipalities are slowly becoming aware of the revenue potential from charges. One way to illustrate the relative growth in charges is to look at movement in the fee intensity. The fee intensity is simply the ratio of fees to each dollar of taxes. Both fee and tax revenue have been growing, but if fees are growing faster than taxes, then the fee intensity is rising. A greater reliance on tax revenue, in contrast, would show up as a decline in the fee intensity. The fee intensity for total charges has shown a cyclical pattern over the past twenty years, but this pattern is due largely to fluctuations in public utility charges (figure 2).

When the fee intensity for current charges is considered separately, a pattern of relatively steady growth emerges. Municipalities are gradually placing more emphasis on public prices. If this trend continues, what impact will it have on future revenues?

PROJECTING LOCAL GOVERNMENT REVENUE

In the last decade a number of projections have been made on the state and local sectors of the economy.[11] A period of steady growth in state and local expenditures has forced public officials to consider fiscal planning for the future. There also is an increased awareness of the development roles played by the public sector — most notably in highways, water supply, energy supply, education, and airports. Through the use of projections public officials can adapt continuously to economic events that affect revenue sources rather than change policies only after the full force of the impact is realized.

Many researchers have examined the way that tax revenue changes in response to changes in other economic variables.[12] But the question what happens to revenue if municipalities turn to stronger reliance on public prices has received less attention. We used a regression model similar to models in previous studies, except for the inclusion of a fee intensity variable, to make revenue projections to the year 2000.[13] Figure 3 illustrates the close relationship between the actual and predicted values of municipal general revenue during the 1955-1976 period.

To make projections for the year 2000 requires an estimate of the independent variables. The MIT-PENN-SSRC (MPS) model of the U.S. economy has produced estimates of real income and prices. Real income per capita in 1967 dollars is projected to rise from

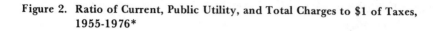

**Figure 2.   Ratio of Current, Public Utility, and Total Charges to $1 of Taxes,
1955-1976***

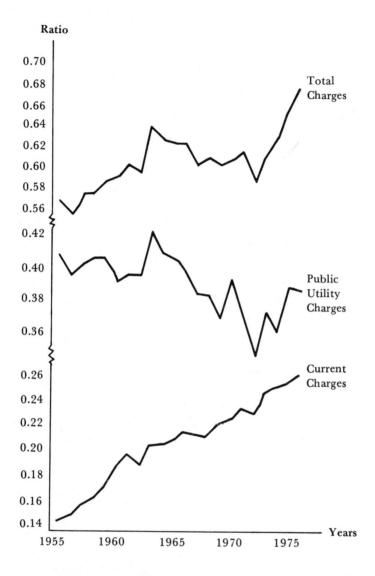

---

*   Current charges are amounts received from the public for goods and services
    benefiting the person charged (excluding public utility charges). Total charges
    is the sum of current charges, , public utility charges, and liquor store revenue.

Figure 3. **Actual and Predicted Growth in General Revenue for Municipalities, 1955-1976**

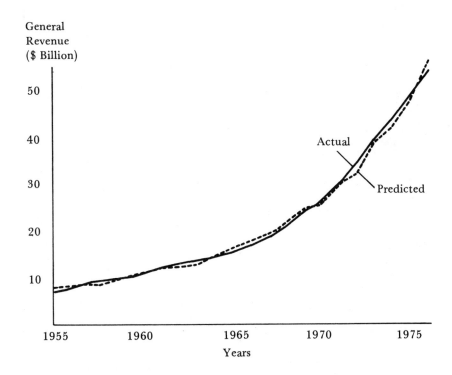

$3750 in 1976 to $7345 in 2000. Lagged prices, where 1967 is the base year, will rise from an index number of 147.7 in 1975 to 368.5 in the year 1999. It is more difficult to obtain projections of the other independent variables such as federal aid and fee intensity, so various scenarios are illustrated (table 1). One scenario assumes no change in the share of intergovernmental aid and the share of taxes, excluding property and sales taxes, but lets the fee intensity (for current charges) vary from the 1976 level of 0.265 to 0.50. The other scenario allows for an increase in the share of grants from 40 percent to 50 percent.

Table 1 illustrates that general revenue foregone by cities in the year 2000 will be of the magnitude of $101.9 to $116.8 billion, depending on the aid share, if the fee intensity ratio does not rise from 0.265 to 0.50. The potential of user charges as a revenue source

Table 1.   Projections of City Government General Revenue for Year 2000 (in millions)

	No change in share of tax revenue (excluding property and sales taxes) and no change in share of aid	No change in share of tax revenue (excluding property and sales taxes); but share of aid is increased from 40 to 50 percent
No change in fee intensity	$ 271,382	$ 311,078
Fee intensity increases from 0.264 to 0.50	373,303	427,908

Note: These projections are based on results from regression analysis and are reliable insofar as the regression model is correctly specified.

and a policymaking tool has been largely untapped. These revenue projections should be taken as an indication of the opportunities available to local governments for greater reliance on user charges to finance government services.

One limitation of the simple regression analysis is that the growth in revenue bonds was not considered. This method of local government financing fosters greater reliance on public prices because pure revenue bonds are secured solely through user charges. The July 31, 1978, issue of *Business Week* indicated that experts see opportunities for more revenue bond financing with the passage of Proposition 13. If this expectation is correct, more reliance on user charges will certainly occur. Banks, under a section of the Glass-Steagall Act, are not allowed to underwrite revenue bonds. But they have already stepped up their lobbying efforts to reverse this section of the act because of expectations that the revenue bond market will be booming soon.

There are several favorable aspects of a shift toward more revenue bond financing. Revenue bonds secured by user fees should encourage greater attention to efficiency because local government enterprises will have to meet the demands of participants in two separate markets — consumers and bond holders. Another favorable aspect is that prices will be charged for use of equipment. Currently many user charges cover operating costs but neglect capital costs. Revenue bond financing will facilitate setting appropriate prices that include both operating costs and rent for capital equipment or facilities.

This model demonstrates in a rough sense the revenues that could be available through use of public prices and user fees. Projecting increased revenues would mean also projecting increased expenditures, but that is not our point. We are talking about a mix of revenues from different sources to finance services that citizens want. Many services that are now financed through general taxation such as the property tax could be financed more efficiently and equitably through user fees. General taxes could be used to finance truly collective goods and services.

Action on Costs: The Occasion for Improved Personnel Management

Thus far we have concentrated mainly on the tax and revenue aspects of the Proposition 13 movement. However reductions in revenues require reductions in government costs. Correspondingly, lower costs mean less revenue is required. Thus action on the costs of government is also a central part of governments' response to the current demands of the citizenry. In the first section we briefly described some of the economic constraints on governmental action to reduce costs. In this section we want to focus on an aspect of cost for which governments have considerable flexibility to achieve reductions — personnel costs.

Perhaps governments could have recognized the sentiments of the taxpayers sooner and taken more effective action earlier to reduce expenditures. This issue is now beside the point, at least with respect to California governments. They now face the necessity of reducing expenditures. And the largest single item in their expenditures is personnel costs — the salaries and benefits of people who work for government. In some cases personnel costs make up as much as 85 percent of the operating budgets of local governments, although the average is below that. In any discussion of cost reductions personnel costs deserve central consideration.

LAYOFFS AND FREEZES

Unfortunately most of the debates about Proposition 13 before and immediately after its passage implied that the only two ways of cutting or holding down personnel costs are general layoffs (reducing the size of the work force through direct separation of workers) and across-the-board freezes (on pay and benefits, on hirings). The California state legislature's plan for allocating the more than $5 billion state surplus to localities included several important conditions. One is that all local jurisdictions are required to freeze salaries for fiscal year 1978-1979. That prospect is not very appealing to public employees or to the unions that represent them.[14] Furthermore many California jurisdictions have reportedly instituted hiring freezes and effected some layoffs. Such actions can be characterized most optimistically as stopgap measures, and they hold the seeds of problems at least as severe as those they are intended to solve, especially if they are maintained for any length of time.

Government officials must not delude themselves that a hiring and promotion freeze, for example, is an efficient solution to any but the briefest revenue shortfall. It is almost axiomatic to point out that a hiring and promotion freeze, if prolonged, results in the employer's loss of the best employees and retention of the worst. Government salaries overall are relatively good, and the inferior worker is not likely to better his financial lot elsewhere. However, public sector salaries for top managers and technical specialists are often only barely competitive with those of the private sector. Faced with the prospect of no promotion and no opportunity to obtain a better job in government, the best managers and specialists are likely to look elsewhere. And good jobs are usually available for highly capable workers.

The same principle operates in the case of salary freezes. The highest performers know their own wage-earning capability and, facing the prospect of long periods with no pay increases, will depart the government and find better pay in another job. Another problem with salary freezes is the potential for wide-scale worker unrest and dissatisfaction. When an entire class of government workers is getting no pay increases while their peers in the private sector and at other levels of government are receiving increases, the stage is set for exceedingly harsh relationships, perhaps including militant unionism and damaging labor actions such as strikes.[15]

PERSONNEL MANAGEMENT ALTERNATIVES

We do not intend to argue that layoffs and freezes are not valid management tools to cut costs in the short run — they are. However, governments that are considering those measures need to compare them with alternative, and perhaps more efficient, methods. In practice such assessment is not always easy.

Most local governments already have a specific plan or procedure for reducing the work force (sometimes as a layoff provision in union contracts). Since the procedure exists, it is relatively easy to use. Similarly in the case of hiring, promotion, or salary freezes, one action by the chief administrative officer or elected council is usually sufficient. Other alternatives have generally not been established, and coming up with them requires creativity, analytic capability, and receptivity to change.

One source of new ideas is the work force itself. In any government there are numerous people with a wealth of ideas for cutting costs. For example, when they have asked employees, jurisdictions have discovered that some workers would be willing to work fewer hours a week, with reduced total pay, to have more time to pursue other interests. For some kinds of jobs alternatives to the traditional forty-hour work week are feasible, without substantially reducing services.

There are frequently lower-cost ways of doing traditional jobs. In Alexandria, Virginia, for example, the police department has a program to allow for the conversion of certain non-law-enforcement jobs to civilian status. In some divisions many jobs that used to be done by uniformed police personnel are now done by civilian employees at lower cost. For instance, dispatchers are nonuniformed, as are records clerks and some employees in planning and research. There are two basic, long-run results of this effort: (1) More uniformed police officers are engaged only in law enforcement activities. (2) The essential record-keeping, dispatch, and planning tasks can be performed at lower cost because of the salary and pension differentials between uniformed and nonuniformed employees. In effect the city's total personnel cost for a civilian worker in the police department is about half that for a uniformed police officer.

Some jurisdictions have used a technique called broad-banding (a job classification term) to achieve greater efficiency. Worcester, Massachusetts, for example, had separate inspection units to handle construction inspections, building inspections for code violations, and residential inspections. A new code inspections department was established to consolidate all inspectional activities and permit the assignment of inspectors to whatever inspectional jobs are required. There are no longer building inspectors, housing inspectors, and construction inspectors who do only those kinds of inspections. Such steps can also produce better services. St. Paul, Minnesota, consolidated most of its licensing bureaus into one office, thereby eliminating duplication and unnecessary functions.

Many local governments have undertaken work-scheduling programs to insure that the greatest numbers of workers are on the job at peak demand times without having to hire additional employees just to handle peak work load. Some such actions have been taken to assure that peak service demands are met following necessary cutbacks in the numbers of available workers. Other jurisdictions have discovered that staffing levels in some service departments were set at the number needed to meet peak work load demands but that those staffing levels were much higher than necessary to carry the normal work load. They then reduced the staffing levels to those required for average work loads (through attrition, reassignments and, occasionally, reductions in force) and made other arrangements, such as temporary reassignments from other departments, to handle heavy work loads when they occur.

These are but a few of the ways that local jurisdictions have cut actual or expected personnel costs without resorting to general layoffs and across-the-board freezes. Some of the programs no doubt have entailed selective reductions in force and hiring freezes to lower the staffing levels through attrition. However, the key word is *selective.* Through analysis of their operations, local governments have zeroed in on the areas where efficient changes can be made.

One of the most promising activities in the management of government personnel has been the establishment in recent years of joint labor-management committees. A number of jurisdictions have set up committees that comprise representatives of management and employee organizations or unions as a nonadversarial forum for solving the complex problems of governments. The National Center for Productivity and Quality of Working Life has been instrumental in fostering some of the labor-management committees and in setting up a network of such committees so that they may share some of their experiences, problems, and solutions.[16]

A NEW LOOK AT PERSONNEL MANAGEMENT

One benefit of the tax-cutting movement — with its obvious requirements to reduce costs and spend its dollars more efficiently — is
that it can provide a powerful incentive for government officials to
take a comprehensive look at the management of their work forces.
Managers and elected officials may well begin to ask whether their
governments' personnel management programs result in the highest
levels of worker performance at the lowest cost.

A guidebook that we published in early 1977 argued that the
fiscal squeeze and the need for greater productivity in government
should be forcing the assessment of personnel management policies, programs, and practices against clearly defined objectives.[17]
We believe that public personnel management programs have been
negatively affected by the misguided notion that their whole purpose
is to ensure merit employment practices. The purpose of personnel
management programs should be to encourage and enhance performance, both of employees individually and of the government as a
whole. Merit is the means of achieving that purpose, and there is no
quarrel with the principles of merit.

Local governments need to determine for themselves what their
personnel management practices are supposed to accomplish — that
is, they must define their objectives — establish realistic measures of
performance, and determine whether the objectives are being
achieved. For example, assuming that at least one of the objectives
of compensation programs is to motivate employees to superior
performance, one might ask whether employees receive merit increases only on the basis of their performance. The answer in many
jurisdictions will be no — employees receive pay increases regardless
of their performance, short of total incompetence. Many similar
questions need to be posed and answered. Such an assessment can
have a significant effect on government's ability to produce services
at lower cost.

The 1977 guidebook was one product of a broad study on
personnel management and productivity in city government, which
involved eight medium-sized cities across the United States. In the
final report on that project we concluded:

> Without doubt, many of the traditional systems, practices,
> and procedures that have grown up around the concept of merit

pose significant barriers to improving government productivity. They especially do not provide adequate incentives to managers to manage well or to employees to perform well . . . . That does not mean that the concepts or principles of merit employment in government should be challenged. Rather, it is meant to challenge the shrouding of incompetence, inflexibility, invalidity, inaccuracy, and unreasonableness in the cloak of merit.[18]

Conclusion

In this paper we have concentrated on two kinds of governmental changes that are potential components of effective government responses to the taxpayer revolt: moving toward greater use of charges and fees for public services and improving personnel management. We see a strong connection between these two positive changes, a connection based on performance.

Much of the attraction of user fees is that if governments do not perform well in providing the priced service, consumers have the option of not purchasing it. Similarly performance should be the primary basis of all actions that a government takes with respect to its employees. Since employees have much to do with all aspects of any given service — its quantity, quality, cost, and timeliness of delivery — it makes good sense to argue that, if the service is priced, then consumers' decision to purchase or not can be an indicator of employee performance. That does not mean that public employees should become salespersons, attempting to entice citizens to purchase the services. It does mean, however, that government workers should become well informed about their market. They should strive to know more about what the citizens want and are willing to purchase, and how they, as service providers, can best meet those demands.

Notes

1. Thomas E. Borcherding and Robert T. Deacon, "The Demand for the Services of Non-Federal Governments," *American Economic Review* 63, no. 5 (December 1972): 894; W. Z. Hirsch, *The Economics of State and Local Government* (New York: McGraw-Hill, 1970).

2. Leif Johanson, *Production Functions* (Amsterdam, Holland: North Holland Publishing Co., 1972), and W. E. G. Salter, *Productivity and Technical Change* (Cambridge, England: Cambridge University Press, 1960).

3. Dick Netzer, *Economics and Urban Problems: Diagnoses and Prescriptions* (New York: Basic Books, 1970), pp. 185-190.

4. The principles of pricing municipal services have recently been discussed in *Public Prices for Public Products*, ed., Selma J. Mushkin (Washington, D.C.: Urban Institute, 1972).

5. A detailed discussion on the efficiency characteristics of user charges is given in Werner Z. Hirsch, *The Economics of State and Local Government* (New York: McGraw-Hill, 1970); and a discussion of ways to maintain equity is given in Selma J. Mushkin and Charles L. Vehorn, "User Fees and Charges," *Governmental Finance* (November 1977); 42-48.

6. For a more complete discussion on the potential for benefits from charging property owners a price to finance the total firefighting operations of city fire departments, see William Pollack, "Pricing Fire Protection Services," in *Public Prices for Public Products*, pp. 307-335; also Erling Mork, "A Fire Service Demand Charge Study" (Tacoma, Washington, January 1976).

7. See the findings of a survey conducted by the NTA Committee on Local Nonproperty Taxation, "User Charges: Their Role in Local Government Finance," prepared by Frederick D. Stocker with the assistance of Marc Posner, *Proceedings of the Sixty-Seventh Annual Conference*, NTA-TIA, 1974, pp. 398-423.

8. Laurence Dougharty et al., "Municipal Service Pricing: Impact on Urban Development and Finance Summary and Overview" (Santa Monica, Calif.: Rand, R-1878/1-NSF, November 1975).

9. Frederick D. Stocker, "Diversification of the Local Revenue System: Income and Sales Taxes, User Charges, Federal Grants," *National Tax Journal* 20 (September 1976): 320.

10. Advisory Commission on Intergovernmental Relations, *Local Revenue Diversification: Income, Sales Taxes and User Charges*, Report A-47, (Washington, D.C., 1974).

11. For example, see Eugene P. McLoon, Gabrille C. Lupo, and Selma J. Mushkin, *Long Range Revenue Estimation*, State-Local Finances Project of the George Washington University, 1967; and Selma J. Mushkin and G. C. Lupo, "Project '70: Projecting the State and Local Government Sector," *Review of Economics and Statistics* 49 (May 1967): 237-245.

12. John Blegler and Perry Shapiro, "The Responsiveness of State Tax Revenue to Economic Growth," *National Tax Journal* 21 (March 1968): 46-56;

Ann F. Friedlaender, Gerald J. Swanson, and John F. Due, "Estimating Sales Tax Revenue Changes in Response to Changes in Personal Income and Sales Tax Rates," *National Tax Journal* 26 (March 1973): 103-110; Gerald E. Auten and Edward H. Robb, "A General Model for State Tax Revenue Analysis," *National Tax Journal* 29 (December 1976): 422-435.

13. The regression was run in double-log form over the period 1955 to 1976. The estimates have been adjusted for first-order autocorrelation, since the Durbin-Watson statistic was quite low when ordinary least squares was applied. The results are

$$\ln GR = \begin{array}{ccc} -1.50 + 0.94 \ln Y + 1.12 \ln CPI_1 \\ (-0.45) \quad (3.23) \quad (6.53) \end{array}$$

$$\begin{array}{ccc} + 0.62 \ln A + 0.50 \ln FI - 0.14 \ln OT \\ (2.45) \quad (2.04) \quad (-0.88) \end{array}$$

$$R^2 = 0.997$$

where the t-values of the coefficient estimates are shown in parentheses and where

GR = general revenue
Y = real per capita income
CPI_1 = consumer price index lagged one year (a measure of last year's inflation experience on this year's budget)
A = percent of general revenue obtained from intergovernmental aid
FI = ratio of current charges to tax revenue
OT = tax revenue other than property and sales taxes as a share of own source revenue (municipal income taxes included in this variable). The coefficient for this variable has a sign contrary to expectations, but is not significantly different from zero. The share actually declined during the late 1950s and early 1960s.

14. See "A Backlash to the Tax Revolt," *Business Week*, July 31, 1978, pp. 69-70.

15. Joanne Omang, "Paying for the Tax Revolt," *Washington Post*, July 2, 1978, p. B1-B2.

16. For reference, see *Directory of Labor-Management Committees*, 2nd ed., (Washington, D.C.: National Center for Productivity and Quality of Working Life, 1978).

17. Selma J. Mushkin, Frank H. Sandifer, and Charles Warren, *Assessing Personnel Management: Objectives and Performance Indicators* (Washington, D.C.: Public Services Laboratory, 1977).

18. Selma J. Mushkin and Frank H. Sandifer, *Personnel Management and Productivity in City Government* (Lexington, Mass.: D.C. Heath, Lexington Books, forthcoming).

Improving the Performance of a Governmental Agency

Rensis Likert
Charles T. Araki

There is widespread concern over the costs of governmental activities and services and the tax burden that these costs impose. Efforts to reduce this burden and lower these costs are being tried. Many of these efforts will be seriously disruptive, particularly those that arbitrarily reduce the quality and quantity of governmental services below the levels that citizens expect and demand.

A much better way to reduce costs and taxes is to improve the productivity and performance of governmental employees through better administration.

This paper will describe briefly a project in the state of Hawaii designed to improve the administration of the State Department of Labor and Industrial Relations. The organizational development effort will be discussed along with quantitative evidence of the improvement obtained in the human component and in performance.

The improvement in management was achieved by helping administrators use a system of management based on the principles and procedures used by business and government managers who achieve 10 percent to 40 percent better performance than average managers, along with better employee satisfaction and labor relations (Likert 1977). This system of management, called System 4 (a participative group model; System 3 is consultative, System 2 is benevolent authoritarian, System 1 is punitive authoritarian; Bowers 1976; Likert and Likert 1976), was derived from rigorous, quantitative research done by the Institute of Social Research of the University of Michigan. Employees doing widely different kinds of work were studied, and data were obtained from every hierarchical level. These studies involved more than twenty thousand managers and two hundred thousand nonsupervisory employees. Over $15 million was spent on this research (Likert 1961; Likert 1967).

Joshua Agsalud became director of the Hawaii State Department of Labor and Industrial Relations in December 1974. To improve the performance of the department and the job satisfaction of its personnel, he discussed in his initial meetings with his division administrators the origin and nature of participative management and encouraged them to try to move their management behavior closer to System 4. Dr. Agsalud recognized that training and other assistance would be needed to help these administrators improve their leadership behavior. With the assistance of Rensis Likert and Charles Araki an organizational development program was made available. The Employment Service Division and the Enforcement Division were the first to use this resource. An organizational development project was conducted with them during the period September 29, 1976, to September 15, 1977.

This organizational development project employed a particularly effective method for achieving better performance, namely, the survey feedback organizational cycle (Bowers 1973; Bowers and Franklin 1977; Likert and Likert 1976). The activities carried out during the project year to implement each step in the cycle are shown in the appendix to this paper.

The first measurements (T_1) of the human component of these divisions occurred between October 27 and November 5, 1976. The second measurements (T_2) were taken from July 18 to July 22, 1977.

The results of these measurements are shown in table 1 in the form of indexes and mean scores for groups of indexes. The response to individual items in the questionnaire is not shown. The table contains the scores for the T_1 and T_2 measurements, the number of persons involved (No.), and a test of whether the T_2 data are significantly different from the T_1 results or whether random variation might account for the differences. The alternative responses to each questionnaire item were scored from 1 to 5, with 5 being the favorable end of the continuum.

As table 1 indicates, the total scores for organizational climate and for managerial leadership showed statistically significant improvement from T_1 to T_2, that is, they showed shifts toward System 4. Some of the subscores in both organizational climate and managerial leadership, although showing shifts in a favorable direction, did not have differences large enough to be statistically significant. All the measurements of the intervening variables (peer relationships, work group function, and satisfaction) revealed shifts toward System 4, but none of these changes was large enough to be statistically significant.

Leadership and organizational climate are causal variables. Changes in them are followed in time by corresponding improve-

Table 1. Mean Ratings for Organization Survey Profile for First (T_1) and Second (T_2) Measurements by Organizational Variables, Number, t-Test Statistic, Degree of Freedom and Level of Significance, September 1977

Organizational Variables	(T_1) Mean	No.	(T_2) Mean	No.	t-Test Statistic	Df	Level of Significance
Organizational climate (causal variable)	2.761	179	2.910	183	−2.0081	360	0.0454[a]
Motivational level	3.057	179	3.169	183	−1.2370	360	0.2169
Management alertness	2.825	179	2.975	183	−1.7590	360	0.0794[b]
Supervisors open to ideas	2.672	177	2.923	183	−2.8318	358	0.0049[a]
Lateral coordination	2.929	177	2.966	180	−0.3783	355	0.7054
Decision-making process	2.594	179	2.762	182	−1.8678	359	0.0626[b]
Lower-level influence	2.446	178	2.654	181	−2.0838	357	0.0379[a]
Managerial leadership (causal variable)	3.342	179	3.537	183	−1.9382	360	0.0534[a]
Interpersonal support	3.763	179	3.867	183	−0.9979	360	0.3190
Goal emphasis	3.430	179	3.538	182	−1.0153	359	0.3107
Team building	3.111	179	3.446	183	−2.8524	360	0.0046[a]
Work facilitation	3.059	178	3.309	183	−2.2491	359	0.0251[a]
Peer relationships (intervening variable)	3.247	179	3.357	187	−1.2301	359	0.2195
Interpersonal support	3.746	179	3.789	182	−0.5144	359	0.6073
Goal emphasis	3.206	179	3.343	182	−1.4167	359	0.1574
Team building	3.047	179	3.167	182	−1.0663	359	0.2870
Work facilitation	2.990	179	3.118	183	−1.1816	360	0.2381
Work group function (intervening variable)	3.471	179	3.556	183	−1.1151	360	0.2655
Satisfaction (end-result variable)	3.480	179	3.575	183	−1.1600	360	0.2468

[a] Highly significant, greater than the 0.05 level.

[b] Significant up to the 0.07 level.

ment in the other variables. The improvement in the leadership and organizational climate variables can therefore be expected to result in corresponding improvement in motivation, communication, team work, the functioning of the work groups, and performance.

The improvement that occurred in these divisions in their leadership and organizational climate is remarkable because it happened in such a relatively short time, October 1976 to July 1977. (Both divisions showed improvement; the Employment Service Division started with somewhat higher scores and showed slightly greater improvement than did the Enforcement Division.) In most organizations it usually takes longer for measurable improvements to occur. An important factor that no doubt contributed to this rapid improvement was the encouragement that the project received throughout its life from Dr. Agsalud. Dr. Agsalud's own leadership behavior and the organizational climate that this leadership created also contributed to the rapid improvement.

Improved Administration Brings Better Productivity

When measurable improvement — a shift closer to System 4 — occurs in the human component variables, it is typically accompanied by simultaneous or subsequent improvement in performance. Performance data are available for the Employment Service Division in the form of individuals placed per staff-year worked. This is considered a good measure of performance. Table 2 contains these data.

Table 2. Performance Results for Employment Service Division

	FY 74	*FY 75*	*FY 76*	*FY 77*	*FY 78* *(First Quarter)*
Individuals placed per staff-year worked	139	151	200	227	244

As table 2 shows, there was impressive improvement in this important index of performance. The improvement started before the organizational development project was begun and is continuing, as expected, beyond the end of the project. The initial improvement may well have been a result of the response of the administrator of the Employment Service Division to Dr. Agsalud's encouragement of the division administrators to move the management systems of their divisions closer to System 4.

Hawaii's ranking among all states for the performance of the Employment Service Division, as would be expected, also showed an improvement.

These performance results for the Employment Service Division are consistent with the findings in many other organizations. A shift toward System 4 in the human component scores is accompanied or followed by an improvement in performance.

A report on this project to Dr. Agsalud contained the following: In looking to the future, it is important to recognize that there is an opportunity for further improvement in the human component of the Employment Service and the Enforcement Divisions. Such improvement would, of course, bring additional gains in the productivity and performance of these two Divisions. The evidence that there is an opportunity for further improvement is revealed by comparing the mean (arithmetic average) scores on the indexes which measure the key dimensions of the human components of these two Divisions with National norms. The following table shows for these Divisions the mean scores for measurements at T_1 (October, 1976) and T_2 (July, 1977) for major clusters of indexes. The table also shows mean scores for these variables from a National data bank. The data bank means are for 4,532 white collar workers. These are workers in many medium-sized and large U.S. corporations.

Organizational Variable	$\overline{M}(T_1)$	$\overline{M}(T_2)$	$\overline{M}$ (white collar workers)
Organizational climate	2.76	2.91	3.29
Managerial leadership	3.34	3.54	3.71
Peer leadership	3.25	3.36	3.38
Work group function	3.47	3.56	3.69
Satisfaction	3.48	3.58	3.72

An examination of the above table reveals that for these Divisions, improvement occurred in the means from T_1 to T_2 for each of the clusters of indexes shown. The data in the table indicate also that further improvement should be sought. For every cluster of indexes, the T_2 means are below the National norm mean scores for white collar workers. The managers and supervisors in the two Divisions should be encouraged to continue the improvement that they already have shown and they should be provided with training and coaching to assist them in doing so.

Conclusion

This paper has described the way that a governmental agency improved its productivity by assisting its administrators to shift their administrative behavior closer to a superior system of management. The evidence indicates that there are opportunities for further improvement in administrative behavior that would bring additional gains in productivity.

In efforts to improve the productivity and performance of governmental agencies, few steps appear to be as promising and offer as great a potential as helping administrators move closer to a participative group model in their management of the human resources of their agency.

Appendix

The following were the key activities carried out in implementing the survey feedback organizational improvement cycle.

Step 1: Initial measurement of human organizational variables (T_1)

Activities	*Dates*
1. Initial organizational meeting with DLIR project director	29 Sept. 1976
2. Initial orientation meeting with key divisional personnel from Employment Service and Enforcement	7 Oct. 1976
3. Project strategy planning and scheduling with project director	20 Oct. 1976
4. Survey distribution to Employment Service Division	27-29 Oct. 1976
5. Survey distribution to Enforcement Division	1 Nov. 1976
6. Collection of completed surveys from Enforcement and Employment Service divisions	5 Nov. 1976
7. Checking and mailing of completed survey to consultants	8 Nov. 1976

Desired model: System 4 specifications

Activity	
Orientation workshop on System 4 for key personnel of Employment Service and Enforcement Divisions	16-17 Nov. 1976

Step 2: Data analysis and interpretation in terms of desired model

Activity	
Data feedback workshop for work group leaders in the Employment Service and Enforcement Divisions	19-20 Jan. 1977

Step 3: Diagnosis of organization (work group)

Activity

Data analysis and feedback to all work group members by immediate supervisor	21-30 Jan. 1977

Step 4: Developing action plan for organization

Activity

All work groups develop action plans using internal or external consultants as needed	Feb. 1977

Step 5: Action phase

Activities

1. Implementing action plans primarily through the weekly problem-solving meetings of each work group	Mar.-Apr. 1977
2. Seminar to review progress on implementing action plans	May 1977
3. Consultation by consultants	Jun.-Jul. 1977

Step 6: Remeasurement phase (T_2)

Activities

1. Second measurement data collection	18-22 Jul. 1977
2. Data interpretation and analysis	Aug. 1977

Step 7: Final report and evaluation

Activities

1. Final report to director of DLIR	15 Sept. 1977
2. Final feedback seminar (evaluation) with key personnel of DLIR	

References

Bowers, D. G. 1973. O. D. Techniques and Their Results in 23 Organizations: The Michigan ICL Study. *Journal of Applied Behavioral Science* 9(1): 21-43.

Bowers, D. G. 1976. *Systems of Organization: Management of the Human Resource.* Ann Arbor, Mich.: University of Michigan Press.

Bowers, D. G., and Franklin, J. L. 1977. *Survey-Guided Development: Data Based Organizational Change.* La Jolla, Ca.: University Associates.

Likert, R. 1961. *New Patterns of Management.* New York: McGraw-Hill.

Likert, R. 1967. *The Human Organization: Its Management and Value.* New York: McGraw-Hill.

Likert R. 1977. *Past and Future Perspectives on System 4.* Ann Arbor, Mich.: Rensis Likert Associates.

Likert, R. 1978. An Improvement Cycle for Human Development. *Training and Development Journal* 32(7): 16-18.

Likert, R., and Likert J. G. 1976. *New Ways of Managing Conflict.* New York: McGraw-Hill.

Part Four
An Exchange on the
Public's View of Proposition 13

An Exchange on the Public's View of Proposition 13

Warren Mitofsky (CBS News): If there was one issue in Campaign '78, it was the pocketbook. California voters said that resoundingly when they voted almost two to one to cut property taxes. The same day Ohio voters said it in defeating emergency school tax proposals in both Cleveland and Columbus, raising the real possibility that schools might not operate.

New Jersey voters said it in rejecting Senator Clifford Case's bid for a fifth term, nominating instead a Reagan Republican who campaigned on a platform of sharp tax reduction.

But the message came most loudly from California where the tax question, Proposition 13, caused what may be a record voter turnout in a primary. Within minutes after the polls closed, they were dancing in the San Fernando Valley, the Los Angeles suburb where the tax revolt began. Howard Jarvis's Proposition 13 had won in a landslide.

The next day Jarvis warned, If lawmakers don't cut out waste in bureaucracy, they're in for more trouble. He said, "November's just around the corner, I've got another amendment. It's to freeze the sales tax and the income tax January 1, 1979."

The message from California resounded quickly across the country. President Carter discussed it at a White House breakfast with House leaders. Indiana's John Brademas said it underscored the need for a major tax reduction by Congress this year. The president's chief inflation fighter, Robert Strauss, called it a lesson for all federal, state, and county governments. People want more efforts in efficient administration, he said.

Senate Democratic leader Robert Byrd called the vote "a message for everybody." And his Republican counterpart, Howard Baker, said that if Republicans don't run on it, they're "political idiots."

There were those, too, who wondered where the money would come from for government services that have come to be regarded as essential.

The head of the National League of Cities, Alan Beals, expressed concern about the ripple effect. Beals believes that the citizens may have second thoughts when they see the reality of the cutback in services.

CBS News conducted a poll for its Los Angeles station, KNXT, and the Los Angeles *Times.* It was a random sample of almost twenty-five hundred Californians across the state. They were interviewed right after they voted on June 6. Was the vote in California a tax revolt? According to supporters themselves, most voted for Proposition 13 simply to lower property taxes. I find it hard to believe that people would not vote for any tax cut. Two of five indicated that the initiative was a way to show the politicians what the people want. Only one in five thought the government provided too many unnecessary services, and very few indicated that their vote was influenced either by television ads or by their choice for governor.

Most did not believe warnings about reduced services. The proposition was probably primarily a way to reduce taxes.

Opponents of the initiative seemed to be motivated primarily by fear of loss of services and possible increases in other taxes. One in ten who voted against the proposition feared that they would lose their job, and an equal number specified the lack of clear assistance for renters in Proposition 13. Witness the current state of affairs in San Diego and Los Angeles where renters are protesting the lack of reduction in rent that they've received since the Jarvis amendment was passed.

Whether you are a Republican or a Democrat, a high school dropout or a college graduate, make less than $8,000 a year or more than $25,000, are under or over fifty — if you went to the polls in California on June 6, you probably voted for Jarvis. Some groups had been considered more likely than others to vote against the tax-limiting initiative and some of them did. But even the few groups that seemed to have a clear self-interest in voting no on 13 did so by very narrow margins.

Most people who rent their homes voted no, but more than 45 percent of the renters voted yes.

Although Proposition 13 was widely expected to bring cutbacks in public jobs, over 40 percent of those with public employees in their families voted for it.

Blacks, as expected, voted on balance against it, but over 40 percent of those blacks who voted on Proposition 13 voted yes.

Conservatives, as expected, voted overwhelmingly for it, by a margin of over four to one. But moderates voted nearly two to one for it, and even among liberals more than 40 percent voted yes.

One reason for the overwhelming support among so many groups for the proposition may well be that few of its supporters expected that any of the bad things forecast by its opponents would actually happen. Most 13 supporters did not foresee any hike in other taxes; most didn't expect a cut in municipal services.

Asked what cuts they would favor, if cuts were necessary, most of the voters interviewed by CBS News had few to suggest. The only item that drew majority support on reduction was welfare. Less than 10 percent of local taxes goes to welfare, usually as health services, at least in California.

About a third supported cuts in parks, museums, or recreational facilities. For anything else, less than 20 percent favored any cuts. Some of the most costly services, sanitation, police and fire protection, all found less than 4 percent of the voters willing to support a reduction. About a quarter of today's voters — all the June 6 voters — were opposed to cutbacks on any services, even if necessary.

One thing that was clear in the poll was that voters saw a big difference between Proposition 13 and Proposition 8. For nearly all voters it was either one or the other. Nearly three-quarters of those who voted for Proposition 13 voted against Proposition 8. Almost nine of every ten voters who voted no on Proposition 13 voted yes on Proposition 8.

Proposition 8 was an enabling piece of legislation that would have permitted redistribution of state funds and would have reduced taxes to both renters and owners but not to businesses.

If they had both passed, Proposition 13 would have superseded Proposition 8. So there were two clear, distinct groups voting for 13 and 8.

If supporters of the Jarvis initiative saw no ill effects on services and other taxes, opponents of Proposition 13 did. Over three-quarters of them thought that local services would be reduced, and even more feared that other taxes would rise. The message seems clear: Cut taxes, don't reduce my services, reduce welfare.

But as John Mack of the Urban League said, "People use welfare as being synonymous with black people and, to that extent, there was a dimension of racism expressed in this election. That's a regrettable kind of situation because, for one thing, there are more white people on welfare than there are black people."

Proposition 13 is having an effect on gubernatorial politics in California. Until a few days before June 6, Governor Brown campaigned as one of the biggest critics of Proposition 13. In an April 1978 speech he called Proposition 13 a tax trap. Six months later, or maybe a year after it passes, he said, the government will inevitably have to add new taxes, either at the local level or at the state level. But one day after the vote, Jerry Brown went back to the same voters who overwhelmingly voted for Proposition 13 to seek their support in the general election. Brown, the opponent of 13, sounded as if he had helped draft the tax-relief measure.

He said that he had started out four years ago in a spirit of austerity and frugality, that the voters wanted more of that spirit, that they wanted that spirit of frugality from Sacramento to San Diego to the Oregon border, and he would do his best to carry it out.

So, Governor Brown, the subject of endless presidential speculation, had to do some fence mending to win reelection as governor. On the other hand, some observers are already saying that if Proposition 13 works, Jerry Brown may wind up running for the White House in 1980 on none other than the success of Proposition 13.

Bud Lewis (Roper Organization): Will Rogers used to say that whenever Congress was in session he'd get the same feeling he got when the baby got hold of a hammer. I'm not suggesting that the California voters got hold of a hammer on June 6, but there is a similarity in the vigor and perhaps the marksmanship with which they delivered their views. A number of us since then have spent a lot of time trying to put the pieces together and see whether we can figure out what really happened.

Is there a tax revolt in California? Well, of course, Californians would like to have their taxes cut. But there's something strange about this tax revolt, if there is one. In June, shortly after the primary, we conducted a poll that asked, Over the past year what effect would you say inflation has had on your standard of living? Would you say it has seriously lowered your standard of living, has had some effect but not much, or would you say your standard of living has stayed the same or gone up?

I don't think it is surprising that 21 percent of Californians said that their standard of living had been seriously affected by inflation. But it is surprising that those who voted for Proposition 13 and those who voted against Proposition 13 both claimed to be equally damaged by inflation. So their reason for voting for Proposition 13 is not inflation.

Why indeed did they vote for Proposition 13? We asked another question in which we presented five statements that different people have made about Proposition 13 and asked the respondent to name one or two that seemed to be the best arguments in favor of Proposition 13.

1. If it weren't for inflation, I wouldn't mind property taxes so much.
2. Proposition 13 will force the government to cut out a lot of programs I don't approve of.
3. It's time the politicians learned that they can't do anything they want to.
4. It's not just property taxes; all taxes are too high.
5. Proposition 13 will force the government to cut out a lot of waste and inefficiency.

The reason chosen by most people who voted for Proposition 13 (43 percent of those who voted for 13) was that Proposition 13 would force government to cut waste and inefficiency. If this is a tax revolt, we have something else here.

The second most popular reason (39 percent) was that it was time for politicians to learn that they can't do anything that they want to.

Significantly, the one chosen least was inflation; only 12 percent of the people said inflation.

So something other than just a tax revolt is going on.

We asked another question: Do you think that the politicians are making an honest effort to carry out the will of the people on Proposition 13, or do you think they're trying to change it around to make things the way they want it?

We found that only 25 percent of the people in California think that the politicians are trying to carry out the will of the people; of course, 63 percent of them said that politicians are trying to change things around to be the way they want it.

I had a little trouble with that question. Anybody who writes a question wonders, Did I load that? And somebody remarked that the question used the word *politicians,* and everybody hates politicians. So I decided to put that question in the next poll but to change it to *government officials.*

By the time I got to putting that in, Governor Brown had already performed his masterpiece of acquiescence. He had presided over the distribution of $5 billion to local governments. Indeed, when we polled and asked people what Governor Brown's position was on Proposition 13, 41 percent of the people said he was for it, despite his statements just before the election.

In the poll we took in August 1978, only 19 percent of the people thought that public officials were willing to carry out the will of the people.

There seems to be a kind of cynicism here that we have touched with Proposition 13 and which goes beyond a mere tax revolt. The people are looking at their government. The people who voted for Proposition 13 and the people who voted against Proposition 13 all think that the public officials are going to make the changes that the politicians want and not carry out the will of the people.

I'm not going to claim that Proposition 13 does not have an element of racism. We asked people what they thought would be the result of it, and the people who voted for Proposition 13 denied emphatically that blacks and other minorities would suffer most; that, they said, was not their intention. Welfare is the one public service that anybody knows about that has millions of dollars involved in it and in which they think there's a lot of waste and inefficiency. Moreover, the people who voted for Proposition 13 were not renters. The majority of blacks are renters. The people who came out to vote were home owners, people of upper income, people who had a more conservative point of view and never liked the welfare state anyway.

Is there a lesson in Proposition 13 for public servants? First, Proposition 13 is an intractable issue. The data don't seem to show that anybody can do anything with it. It's a kind of steamroller, monolith, juggernaut force that's coming along. The politicians didn't create this issue. It isn't a manipulative issue. The politicians had nothing to do with Proposition 13, and they still don't know how to handle it.

I was so surprised when I looked at the data for the first time to realize it's just like it was in 1976 when we were polling about

Jimmy Carter and we would ask questions like: Do you think it would be a good thing if the next president didn't spend his political career in Washington? Jimmy Carter was seen in those days, you remember, as a manager, as a pragmatist, a man who'd get things done, rather than an idealist or an issue-oriented person. I happen to think that, partly because of that fact, his rating has been such a disappointment. Many people really wanted him to straighten out the mess in Washington.

At any rate, I would say that almost every demographic description is cynical, convinced that government is not only irresponsible but unresponsive and that there is waste going on in government. The people want to have their cake and eat it. They want their taxes to go down and they want to keep the services which they are committed to. There's no taking away social security from the people. As a matter of fact, they would like to extend it. They want health insurance, by overwhelming majorities. They don't want their taxes to take so much of their disposable income. So the only solution is to cut waste and inefficiency, which may or may not exist to the extent that people think it does.

These people, I think, will vote for tax ceilings, they will vote for spending ceilings, they'll vote for hiring ceilings, anything that will force public administrators to cut the waste and be efficient.

In one poll we asked, Which candidate for governor do you think is more likely to cut waste in government and make it run more efficiently, Jerry Brown or Evelle Younger? Among the people who thought Jerry Brown would cut out waste and run the government more efficiently, Brown won by a margin of 75 points; among the people who thought Evelle Younger would be more efficient, Younger won by a margin of 72 points.

So to anybody who wants to run for office, I would suggest that the best program is active, continuous, public efficiency and good management.

Alan Baron (Baron Reports): A set of statistics and a set of polling results can be used to prove almost anything. That is always the case, I guess. But when the question is varied slightly or the sample is varied slightly, the results on any set of issues vary a great deal.

There have not been any radical changes recently in American viewpoints on basic issues. Americans have always been essentially conservative when asked in the abstract what the role of government should be and whether they favor large government or small government.

In four surveys taken between 1956 and 1964 the Survey Research Center asked whether the government should leave electric power and housing to private business. The public consistently preferred private industry by a two-to-one margin. And when asked whether the federal government should be required to balance its budget, 78 percent now agree with that, compared with 70 percent during the height of the New Deal, during Roosevelt's administration. So the desire to keep government small in the abstract has held fairly constant for many years. People prefer private industry.

The second trend, which is certainly more pronounced now but also has been apparent earlier, is the belief that government is wasteful and inefficient and that politics, or politicians at least, are often corrupt or at least wasteful. This belief has been particularly evident in the last few years in American politics. Ed Koch in New York was leading when he ran for mayor. Then he won the Democratic nomination and the election was all over. The polls showed Koch ahead by twenty points, and then he ran in the general election. Mario Cuomo remained on the ballot, on the liberal ticket, and Cuomo did not conduct a major campaign during that period. Day after day Koch was being endorsed by all those in the political establishment who had originally opposed him for the nomination. The unions were endorsing him, the business groups were endorsing him, all the interests were endorsing him. Finally, Koch's pollster went to his campaign manager and said, Stop. Every time the voters see that somebody else endorsed Ed Koch he drops another percentage in the polls. By election day Koch won by 7 percent or 8 percent over Cuomo. But the voters were becoming convinced that Koch was one of the politicians, and they were moving away from him.

I understand from observers in Maryland politics that the same thing may have happend to Ted Venetoulis, who ran against Blair Lee. Venetoulis started to pick up some momentum. The AFL-CIO endorsed Venetoulis, and that was a great victory. This group endorsed Venetoulis, that group endorsed Venetoulis. The voters were confronted with Lee, the frontrunner, who was endorsed by probably half of the politicians and interest groups. They were confronted with Venetoulis, who was endorsed by the other half of the politicians and interest groups. They were confronted with an unknown, who was endorsed by the Baltimore *Sun*. In probably the most stunning political upset of the year, they voted for the unknown.

That upset speaks not simply of waste and inefficiency in management but to a belief that it's better to shake things up. This attitude was evident in Jimmy Carter's election and is evident again and again in the decline of the political institutions that are normally stabilizers. Clearly voters feel that the political establishment is against them.

When you go beyond the abstract questions and ask specific questions, then the public gives a much different answer. When you ask about health care, when you ask about education, the majority of the public favors increasing government spending for helping the elderly, reducing air pollution, developing greater energy self-sufficiency, making college possible for deserving young people, coping with drugs and addicts, supporting and improving public schools, and improving medical and health care. Between 72 and 81 percent of the public have said there should be no reductions in programs for helping the unemployed, providing adequate housing, providing mass transportation, rebuilding rundown sections of cities and improving the situations of black Americans. No less than 63 percent said that spending for the purpose of helping the poor with welfare programs should not be reduced.

In other words, those who want less government spending and less inefficiency and waste want the same or more government services.

Those who deplore waste and inefficiency in government, who dislike the bureaucracy and think that the politicians are cheating us, come predominantly from the lower socioeconomic groups; these are the poor people, the blacks, the low-income groups. They are the ones who have the least confidence in the political establishment or the politicians who are running the country. At the same time, they are the ones who most agree that government should provide more services to help people. The federal government was rated highly by 32 percent of the college-educated people in polls, but its good rating dipped to 21 percent of high school graduates and to 15 percent of those without a high school diploma.

On the other hand, it is the best-educated and highest-status Americans who are most strongly opposed to government in principle and most likely to oppose government programs.

A 1976 sample asked, How much influence and power should the federal government have? Thirty percent of those without high school diplomas said the federal government should have less power and influence. This rose to 47 percent among high school graduates and to 63 percent among the college educated.

So you've really got two sets of opinions, but the lower socioeconomic groups, the groups that are more likely to vote Democratic, are at the same time more alienated from the system and also more supportive of government programs.

Beyond public opinion what is happening in the country now is a tremendous reaction. Liberal Republicans like Cohen in Maine are supporting Kemp-Roth to cut the federal taxes 30 percent. There is a whole trend in this direction. California started a whole phenomenal movement.

At the same time very traditional conservatives, with a great deal of political logic, are attempting to use this spirit and this movement to justify their positions. Senator Carl Curtis of Nebraska, who has voted against just about every federal program in thirty years, did not run for reelection in 1978 because the polls showed him in serious trouble. He says that he has now been vindicated — that all his votes over the last thirty years against every federal program, except those involved in national defense, have been proven right and that the public now agrees with him.

Just a few years ago Gene McCarthy was doing very well in the primaries in 1968; liberals were being elected, the public was turning against the war in Vietnam. A number of people — and I was one of them — assumed that America was lurching leftward every time a poll said that Americans were alienated and frustrated with the way things were going and that Americans wanted to get out of the war in Vietnam. We believed we were on the verge of a new society and that Michael Harrington was going to prevail.

I don't think Michael Harrington or William Buckley or anyone else has been on the verge of prevailing on these issues. Politics, at least from a candidate's standpoint, goes far beyond the results of polls.

One can argue that Ronald Reagan beats Jimmy Carter in the polls, and one can talk about a conservative trend. But Edward Kennedy beats Ronald Reagan by more than Ronald Reagan beats Jimmy Carter, and Edward Kennedy is hardly a conservative.

One can argue that in Minnesota Bob Short called for a $100 billion cut in the federal budget, and one can say that Minnesota Democrats are becoming conservative. No doubt that helped Bob Short when he defeated Don Fraser, but Fraser was on the wrong side of certain other issues — recreation and environment and abortion. Minnesota's open primary and the 20 percent of the voters who were Republicans in the Democratic primary also helped Short win. Finally, Fraser decided not to adjust local positions to local trends. Fraser took strong positions on national issues. He didn't adopt certain positions to please his local constituency.

It's easy to jump to broad conclusions. It's easy to conclude from one election that the country is moving in a given direction. We have to be cautious of such generalization.

An Exchange on Polling and Poll Results

James Vanecko (Abt Associates Inc.): We're talking about something that is not really new; it has in many ways existed for a long period of time. And different questions produce different results. But since the late forties, at least, some questions have been consistently repeated. For most questions there is remarkable consistency over thirty years. In the midst of that consistency one set of items has been repeated in national polls by the Survey Research Center at Michigan and by other polling organizations since 1948 relating to trust in government.

On some of the issues relating to people's beliefs that government officials and the government will do the right thing, there was remarkable consistency from 1948 to 1967. Seventy-five percent of the American people believed that government would do the right thing. From 1967 into the seventies there has been a dramatic shift in public opinion. The proportion of people believing and trusting in the government has gone down from 75 percent to about 20 percent.

That information has been available since the late sixties. Why didn't we know more about that? Why wasn't there more anticipation of the phenomenon represented by Proposition 13 and some of the shifts that are going back and forth now?

Mr. Baron: I think that the percentage of people who clearly have no faith in government has been going up. I think that the percentage of people who have faith in business has also been dropping. I think that the percentage of people who have faith in organized labor and in virtually all of the institutions in society has dropped.

I don't know what that means. I went to a luncheon in New York at which Lou Harris spoke. Harris was saying that the percentage of people who have confidence in journalists has dropped from 61 to 31 and the percentage of confidence in ministers has dropped from 68 to 42. He was going down a long list. When he finished Gene McCarthy asked whether he had anything on dentists.

In government in the last several years, with Watergate and Vietnam, there were some signs of this declining confidence. The votes for George McGovern and for George Wallace expressed the same disenchantment.

The clearest evidence of this disenchantment comes from the South, where unknown businessmen who have never held office are running in statewide elections. In Alabama this year, a man who will probably be elected governor or certainly has a good shot at it, has never held office before. People are looking for people, for nonpoliticians. Carter's the best example.

So I think that that feeling has been evidenced. The question is, What do you do once you get in office? Like Carter, you're forced to use a lot of tools and methods that aren't really applicable in winning elections. But the system has disintegrated, and the parties don't really mean anything. I think the confidence questions mirror this.

The question for politicians is how to exploit that loss of confidence. Politicians have been trying to do it for a long time, and I think that McGovern and Wallace and McCarthy, to some extent, and Robert Kennedy were all doing that.

Mr. Lewis: Another factor has to do with the economy. When the economy is going down and looks shaky, when people consistently hear that things will be worse next year, then their confidence in all kinds of institutions goes down.

Mr. Mitofsky: People have been lied to for years. They were lied to in Vietnam, they were lied to by a president, they're lied to by the CIA, the FBI, all kinds of institutions. Now we ask them to trust us, the public officials. But they've had reason to wise up and now they're smarter.

Mr. Baron: I saw two questions in a survey dealing with governmental protection of consumers that showed the lack of faith in government, lack of trust in institutions. One question said essentially, If the government wasn't around to check on these big companies, they would be ripping us off a lot more. And everybody agreed.

In the same survey they said, During the last few years the government has adopted a lot of regulations that affect big business and how it deals with consumers, but the businessmen have figured out how to get around them and they're taking more advantage of the people than they used to. And everybody agreed with that too.

They didn't trust either government or business.

Charles Levine (Institute for Urban Studies, University of Maryland): To what extent do you think that people really understand a complex government dealing with a complex social world? Waste and inefficiency may be essential. As someone once said, somebody's red tape is somebody else's procedures. This is a multigoal government, which is a government trying to do something other than deliver the most service at the least cost. That means you're going to have a lot of countervailing and costly goals to meet simultaneously.

To what extent do people in California or around the country understand that? We in academia have not educated people about that idea. We have a very simple-minded model of government.

What kind of model are people out there carrying in the back of their heads about what government is and ought to be?

Mr. Lewis: At the beginning it wasn't at all certain that Proposition 13 would win. There was a great deal of undecided sentiment on the subject, and the legislature put together Proposition 8. It was an alternative, in my opinion a very reasonable alternative to the meat-axe approach of Proposition 13. It used part of the surplus, it returned about half of the property taxes that Jarvis would have, and it protected home owners rather than business. With Proposition 13 business property taxes also go down, and Jarvis works for the real estate board.

At about the same time that Proposition 13 could have lost, a lot of the tax assessors in Southern California began to send out the new assessments for property; some were 100 or 150 percent higher than they had been two years before. This happened at a time when the public knew that there was a sizable surplus. Even Jerry Brown was saying, We're going to have to raise taxes. The people knew there was money there; suddenly everybody said, Where have I heard all that before?

Theoretically people could have hedged their bets and voted for 13 and 8 so that if one didn't pass the other might. But they didn't. They just decided to vote for 13. Ever since, sentiment in favor of Proposition 13 has continued to rise in California. It's now higher than it ever was. A number of people who voted against it are now for it — because its supporters were right. California found $5 billion, cut out another billion, returned $6 billion. And almost no public services are being cut and almost no budgets are being cut.

So how sophisticated are the voters? I think they may be a lot more sophisticated than we are.

Mr. Baron: In 1972 they had Proposition 1 on the ballot in California, which would have cut taxes—not as much as Proposition 13— but it was a long, detailed tax program proposed by Reagan. I asked Reagan why Proposition 1 lost in 1972 and Proposition 13 passed in 1978. Was it strictly a shift in the public? Was Reagan ahead of his time?

Reagan said he thought that the more basic difference was that as the number one advocate of Proposition 1 he was a politician. So Reagan, a politician, a governor supporting Proposition 1, got into an argument with Moretti, the leader on the other side, a Democratic politician who opposed it. In the 1978 election campaign the proposition was being supported by Howard Jarvis, who was not a politician. So he had more credibility than the politicians on the other side. It was the private citizen versus the politicians.

Bruce Long (Advisory Commission on Intergovernmental Relations): The first poll taken on the day of the election said that most people thought they were reducing taxes. A follow-up poll said that most people thought they wanted to reduce services. I wonder if you have any ideas about the reasons for that discrepancy?

Mr. Lewis: This is a good example of a different response to a different question. The waste and inefficiency wasn't included in that question and what that poll found was that people voted for Proposition 13 because they wanted to reduce their property taxes.

Mr. Mitofsky: The main reason that the people who voted for it gave as a reason for their vote was that they thought it was going to lower property taxes. The people who voted against it didn't feel that way. The second reason was that they wanted to show politicians that this is what people wanted. The third reason, way down the list, again among supporters of Proposition 13, was that they thought the government was providing too many unnecessary services.

Mr. Lewis: In the question I had there were two choices. One was that Proposition 13 would force people to cut out a lot of programs I don't approve of, and the other one was that it would force the government to cut out a lot of waste and inefficiency. That's the one they picked.

Mr. Baron: During the last ten years the sales tax has gone up more than the property tax across the country. The sales tax revenues have gone up considerably more.

But any measure of polling that I have seen is that the sales tax is the least objectionable to people and that the property tax is the most. When Richard Nixon was president, he proposed a value-added tax. It's a sales tax at all levels of production, and it's hidden by the time it gets to the consumer. But it can be 20, 25 percent of the cost of what is purchased.

George McGovern and the Democrats jumped on this proposal as regressive. They attacked Nixon and the idea faded away. One reason it faded was that it was attacked from the right. Even though the value-added tax is regressive, it's also hidden and the easiest way to tax people is to tax them by a hidden tax.

The property tax in some cases is added to mortgage payments. If you've paid off your home, you pay it directly. It's much more visible than the sales tax or the income tax.

A law passed in California last year allows a home owner over sixty-five who earns less than $20,000 a year to postpone paying the property tax. When the house changes hands, the state has a lien for the amount of owed property taxes.

This law is equitable because the house is increasing in value, the owner is not getting anything out of it, and the tax comes out of the estate when the capital gain is recognized by the heirs. Very few people agreed to sign up for this program. The idea behind this law was against the ingrained attitude of someone who spent twenty years paying off a house. The person who spends twenty years paying off the mortgage and finally gets the house paid off isn't going to give a lien to the state of California on the house, which is in effect what this tax law did. The idea never sold.

Kathleen McCleery (WETA Public Television, Washington, D.C.): Are there any polls that assess how worried Californians are about 1980, whether people are assured that the funds are going to come through, that the surplus is going to be there, and that the government's going to be there?

Mr. Mitofsky: I don't know directly about the polls, but the Supreme Court in California said that effective January 1, 1980, property taxes couldn't be used for public education. That had already been in effect or had been declared by the court before Proposition 13 was voted on in June. All Proposition 13 did was

speed up by a year and a half the time when that would take effect.

From the proportion of property taxes that go to education, it
was clear that this system would have to be terminated a year and a
half later. So I don't believe that anybody who's thought that
through has been too concerned about the whole thing.

Robin Hickey (National Institute of Education): Are Proposition
13-type issues with fiscal limitations on the ballots in different
states?

Mr. Mitofsky: There are different ways of wording them. Some of
them are spending limitations; some of them are reductions in taxes.
It is not clear yet exactly which ones will stay on and which ones
won't, but there are about fifteen states with some kind of vote.

Dr. Vanecko: A national poll conducted shortly after Proposition
13 found that about two-thirds of the national sample said they
would not want education cut if there was a tax cut. Yet education is the largest expenditure for property taxes.

Is there any further analysis of which public services people
are willing to see cut?

Mr. Mitofsky: This is really from California but I think we had the
same thing in the national poll.

About a fifth of the supporters of Proposition 13 in California
said that they were willing to see cuts in schools. Only 5 percent
of the people who voted against Proposition 13 were willing to make
cuts in schools. Schools are one of the issues that reveal the differences between supporters and opponents. It might tell you who has
more children, the age of the people, or whether they're renters.
I think they're all related. There is a big difference between supporters and opponents of Proposition 13 in terms of their willing-
ness to cut out school money.

The other big difference was street repair. The supporters wanted
it, and the opponents couldn't care less.

Ted Bartell (Applied Management Sciences): Simultaneously with
the campaign there was a big discussion about forced busing in

Los Angeles, in the San Fernando Valley. Most of Jarvis's debates occurred against the president of the School Board of Los Angeles, Howard Miller. Miller kept saying that Proposition 13 would force them to lay off teachers and close down schools. Most of the people who were for 13 were also against busing, and they were just as happy to close the schools as to have their kids bused.

So I'd be curious to know whether your measures were sensitive to an antibusing sentiment as one of the key explanatory variables — at least for the milions of people who live in the San Fernando Valley but, more generally, for Los Angeles — and whether you would have picked that up in the measurements that you conducted.

Mr. Lewis: I never picked it up, but that doesn't say it wasn't there. I polled about busing and I polled about 13, but I never noted any correlation. Improvement in the schools has always been the top Democratic issue in California, partly because of the nature of the constituency of the Democratic party. A lot of disadvantaged people vote Democratic, and they're very interested in schools. Of course, the upper-income people have less confidence in the schools and perhaps don't use them as much.

A Voice: Are the people in California linking spending and power at any point? Are they assuming that they might pay their property tax dollars to local governments and have control at the local level? Or, if property taxes aren't reduced, then they would be paying income tax to the state and there would be a surplus that the state would have to distribute. Is there any linkage there?

Mr. Lewis: No, there isn't and that's been pointed out a number of times. Actually, one of the effects of Jarvis is simply that people will lose a certain amount of local autonomy if they have to go to Sacramento to get money. One of the points that everybody noted is that the vote for Proposition 13 was a conservative vote. Seventy-five percent of all the voters in that primary were home owners, while they account for about 50 percent of California. I'm sure they never meant to give up their local autonomy, but that's the way it seems to be working out.

Erasmus Kloman (National Academy of Public Administration):
How useful is the initiative or referendum as a way of expressing the
will of the people?

Dr. Vanecko: I think it's difficult to figure out the global question you ask about Proposition 13. I don't know whether anyone here is willing to take a stab at it.

Mr. Lewis: I think we're talking about a deep question about representative government. Californians, with their antecedents going
back to Hiram Johnson, have a profound distrust for political institutions. The initiative, referendum, and recall are used extensively
there.

I don't believe that in the long run the initiative has been unsuccessful. It's regrettable that most of them involve million-dollar
campaigns and highly mobilized advertising. But I continue to have
a strong faith in the people, and I think they make up their minds
correctly most of the time.

Mr. Baron: Senator Abourezk has put faith in democracy to the
test because he has proposed a national constitutional amendment
providing for national initiatives. He has some support from some
very conservative people and Abourezk is one of the most liberal
senators. But the objections he's getting now are interesting.

He has a long, detailed paper showing that over the last fifty
years initiatives have been progressive. But Abourezk has not convinced very many liberals that the national initiative is a good idea.
But the initiative is clearly going to be used more and more.

I think its popularity reflects and is related to the decline of
institutions and political parties. It's an opportunity to move outside that framework and to say something.